MULATTO
THE BLACK HISTORY OF CALVERT COUNTY MARYLAND

BY

MICHAEL GAYHART KENT

Pictured : Hezekiah and Ozella Sewell Brooks
The author's Great Grand parents

MULATTO
The Black History of Calvert County Maryland

"The Black History of Calvert County" is intended to convey a double meaning. The goal is to relate the history of people of Color in Calvert County, Maryland and also to illustrate the darkness of the times. The title "Mulatto" is used because the Black and White history of Calvert County is so intermingled. My interest in the subject stems from an oral family history that dates back to 1780 in Calvert County. I have attempted to relay when the history is based on oral recollections and when it comes from written documents.

According to the 1820 Maryland Census, Daniel and Anne Wheeler Kent owned 37 Slaves in the area of Calvert County known as Lower Marlboro. In 1779 the Kents had a son named Joseph who would later become a doctor. Because of a political dispute with another doctor, Joseph left Calvert County. Dr. Kent served in the military before winning a seat in the U.S. House of representatives. Congressman Kent held office from 1810 until he was elected Governor of Maryland in 1826. After Governor Kent's death in 1837, an estate sale was held for the Calvert County property (including Slaves) inherited from his father.

James P. King (1803-1895) purchased two Slaves from the Kent estate sale for his Kingslanding farm, located along the shores of the Patuxent River in Calvert. The Slaves were Henry (1821-1901) and his sister Susan (1822-1881). James P. King fathered three children by Susan. Because Susan did not want to offend the owner's wife, she gave her very" light skinned" mulatto children the last name of Kent. The first born child was my great-grandfather Benjamin Henry Kent (1839-1928). Benjamin's long life enabled him to convey the oral history to his descendants.

Prior to 1850, Susan was given her freedom and 12 acres of land from the King's farm. This was verified by the 1850 census. In 1870, Benjamin married Rachel (1849-1939) a midwife. The two purchased an additional 80 acres from the King farm. They had 16 children, one of whom was my grandfather, Daniel Webster Kent (1883-1966). Daniel, a tobacco farmer married Augusta Brooks (1893-1991) also a midwife and they acquired another 150 acres from the King farm. Daniel and Augusta (Gussie) had 8 children, and an adopted nephew. One of their children was my father, Daniel Webster Gayhart Kent (1914-2014). My father married Viola Russell (1926-2014) and continued to acquire another 125 acres from the old King farm and raised their family of 6 children with the knowledge of the oral history. Mulatto family members are common in the history of many Calvert County families. The theme of this book will be to highlight the opportunities Blacks had to leave Calvert County and why most chose to stay.

The following Table will give the reader an idea of the monetary value placed on Slaves

Slave Valuations in 1841

In the 1840's, citizens were taxed by municipalities on both real (land) and personal property. In order to maintain an equitable taxation throughout Maryland, a schedule was drawn up for Slaves and silver plate. The following schedule was found in a Tax Assessors Field book for Ward 11, in Baltimore Maryland. Information was found in the Baltimore city archives.

The prices at which Slave are to be valued:

Males
From 7 years old to 14 $225.00
  14 "   " " 21 $375.00
  21 "   " " 30 $525.00
  30 "   " " 40 $400.00
  40 "   " " 45 $200.00
  45 "   " " 75 $75.00

Females
From 7 years old to 14 $175.00
  14 "   " " 35 $300.00
  35 "   " " 40 $200.00
  40 "   " " 45 $100.00
  45 "   " " 50 $50.00

Women were valued less than males. Males were most valuable between the ages of 21 and 30 whereas females were most valuable from the ages of 14 to 35.

CHAPTER I
Opportunities for Freedom

Public records show that between 1700 and 1776 about 100,000 slaves were brought to Maryland and Virginia directly from Africa. The mostly male Slaves were used to clear land and plant tobacco. Female slaves were imported for field and domestic work, but also to replenish the workforce. In 1783, the importation of slaves "officially" ended in the state of Maryland. However, by 1800 there were approximately 800 free white, heads of household names in Calvert County's census with almost 4,000 slaves.

The obvious question to ask is how a small group of White people could control so many Slaves? The main factors were superior weapons, organization, and geography. Slaves were most disadvantaged by the geography. The first African Slaves knew how long it took to travel there by sea and relayed that information to their descendants. Slaves did not have anyway of obtaining a ship to leave America and did not have any reason to believe that the rest of the Country was any different than Calvert County.

Part of the superior organization of the Whites was the church. The earliest known church in Calvert County was the Episcopal Church. There has been a large Episcopal Parish in the southern part of the County known as the Christ Church Parish since the 1690's. The churches were built with balconies to accommodate Slaves. Although the institution of Slavery could be morally "justified" by the churches, one wonders how the members could look at the light skinned mulatto children in the balcony and not say anything.

The church promised freedom and eternal happiness after death. In some cases, immediate freedom was offered if the Slave was baptized. Freedom after baptism was conditioned upon the Slave agreeing to leave the state within 30 days of receiving manumission (freedom) papers. Slaves could purchase their freedom by working part time on other farms. The typical work week of a Slave was Monday thru Saturday. On Sunday's they could rest or visit family or hire out to other farms. Another path to freedom was simply to grow old. Slave productivity decreased with age. Females were often freed after their childbearing years ended while males were released about age 50.

Black Slaves were asked to fight in the American Revolution in exchange for freedom. A far greater number achieved freedom during the war of 1812. The British fleet occupied the Chesapeake Bay and the Patuxent River in Calvert County in 1813 and 1814. The British attacked plantations and farms to obtain food, merchandise, and to free Slaves. Freed Slaves could choose to fight for the British, or they could immigrate to Nova Scotia, Bermuda, or the West Indies. Because Black Slaves did not have any knowledge of those places, most chose to stay in Calvert where they knew what to expect. The Treaty of Ghent, which ended the war of 1812, provided for reparations to be paid by the British for the Slaves that fled. In Calvert, 69 owners made claims for 273 slaves. The compensation was $280 per Slave.

CHAPTER II
Slave Life

Charles Ball was born a Slave in Calvert County, Maryland. In 1838, he published a book titled <u>Fifty Years in Chains</u>, or <u>The Life of an American Slave</u>. According to Mr. Ball, Slaves were kept from running away by extreme intimidation. It was easy to intimidate people when they lacked the knowledge of anything or anyone that would help them. Slaves were housed in one room log cabins with a dirt floor. Ball saw as many as 20 at a time living in a small cabin. Slaves might receive one set of clothes a year. Most did not have shoes. There were good masters and bad masters, but it was the overseer who spent the most time with the Slaves. The overseer might rule by intimidation, the whip, or torture. Families were often separated with some allowed to visit on Sundays. After working a full day, Slaves would often garden to supplement their diet.

Prior to the war of 1812, Charles Ball was sold to a Slave trader. Mr. Ball walked from Calvert County, Maryland to South Carolina chained to 50 other Slaves. The trip took four weeks. After arriving in South Carolina, Charles Ball was sold to a plantation in Georgia. After 7 years he escaped and made his way North to Calvert County. This journey took a year. Upon returning to Calvert County, he worked for farmers as a free man. Despite the danger, Ball stayed in Calvert to be near his family. During the war of 1812, Charles Ball volunteered with the Americans. He served as a cook for the sailors who fought the British at St. Leonard Creek in Calvert County. He then traveled with Commodore Joshua Barney during the battles at Bladensburg and Baltimore. After the war, Mr. Ball lived free for years until he was recognized as a fugitive Slave and again sold south. Charles Ball and other runaway Slaves inability to maintain their freedom was later made more difficult by another Calvert County resident. In 1777, Roger B. Taney was born in Calvert County. He would become Chief of Justice of the Supreme Court and write the "Dred Scott Decision" in 1857. "Dred Scott" held that Slaves were property, without constitutional rights, and could be returned to their owners regardless of where they fled. Fortunately, Charles Ball was able to escape again. This time, he was unable find his family, and lived the remainder of his life in Philadelphia.

Another slave with a story that gained national attention was Isaac Brown. Isaac Brown was the Slave of Alexander Somerville in the southern part of Calvert County. In 1845, Somerville was shot in the back by an unknown assailant. Although Isaac Brown was three miles away at the time, he was jailed and convicted. Somerville survived his wound and thought that Isaac Brown had a motive to shoot him. Ten years earlier, Somerville had stabbed and killed Mr. Brown's brother because he returned late from a wedding. Somerville had also reneged on a promise to free Isaac Brown when he turned 35 years old. Mr. Brown was given a 100 lashes, then allowed to heal before being given 100 more lashes. As was the custom, convicted Blacks were sold to Slave traders and Mr. Brown was taken to New Orleans where he would be auctioned further south. Mr. Brown was able to escape to Philadelphia where anti - slavery Quakers protected him and reached out to his family in Calvert. Unfortunately that alerted the Calvert government to his whereabouts and the Governor of Maryland issued a warrant to the Governor of Pennsylvania for Isaac Brown's arrest and return to Maryland. Of course, Slaves did not have Constitutional rights, so double jeopardy did not apply. The Quakers helped Mr. Brown escape to Canada where he became a successful doctor. Dr. Brown's mistreatment became a National story that was widely publicized by the abolitionist movement.

Equality at Sea

Part of the oral history of my family is that a great – great grandfather was a Black merchant seaman who traveled the world. Supposedly, while in the Philippine Islands, this sailor purchased a Japanese wife. Upon returning to the United States, they had a son named Hezekiah Brooks, who was born in 1859. The sailor died shortly thereafter. Hezekiah Brooks appears to look part Asian in his photographs but there is not any other documentation to support this story. The alleged Japanese mother can be found in census reports after she remarried and became Caroline Sims. Hezekiah brooks died in 1922 without leaving any additional evidence of his mother's heritage. Stories of free Black sailors voluntarily returning to the United States during Slavery is supported in a book by Stephen Budiansky titled "Perilous Fight: America's Intrepid War with Britain on the High Seas, 1812 – 1815

Mr. Budiansky asserts that 15% to 20% of American seafarers at that time were free Blacks. Half of the Black seafarers worked in menial roles as stewards or cooks, but the other half were regular seamen, with jobs equal to their White shipmates. The research found that life at sea was an opportunity for equal pay and respect for Free Blacks that did not exist anywhere else in America. "To drive a carriage, carry a market basket after the boss, brush his boots, saw wood and run errands, was as high as a Colored man could rise" on land. But at sea, "the Negro feels as a man" (unidentified Black sailor). Black seafarers responded to the opportunity by sticking with life at sea much longer than Whites. Blacks were on average older (Whites were 16 to 20 years old at enlistment), and more likely to have a wife at the home port. The more experienced Black sailors would often have a higher rank and earn more money than Whites. The average ship owner paid Merchant seaman about $18 per month, but some paid as much as $30 per month. Blacks were almost never made officers, however, commentary from that time period shows an equality and lack of racial animosity among American sailors. On merchant ships and U.S. Navy ships, everyone ate together and worked together. Racial boundaries took a backseat to the rules and regimentation of shipboard life. It is speculated that the stern discipline of shipboard rules for everyone, made race recede in importance. Mr. Budiansky quotes a visitor to a New Orleans seaport who noted with wonder that a Black seaman might "give 20 lashes with the end of a rope to White sailors at sea , but ashore they dare not even look him in the face.

CHAPTER III
Fight for Freedom – The Civil War

While the causes for the Civil War may be debatable, the one point that is undeniable is that the Colored soldiers were fighting for their freedom, the freedom of their families, and our freedom today.

The Emancipation Proclamation became law in January of 1863 and declared the end of Slavery in all states that were in rebellion against the Union. Since Maryland did not secede from the Union, Slavery did not end in Maryland until November of 1864. Calvert County's Colored soldiers who enlisted in 1864 were not released from service until 1867. It is ironic that those who fought for freedom were the last to obtain it.

Bounty Money for Freedom

When the Civil War began in April of 1861, President Abraham Lincoln called for 90-day volunteers. As a result, 75,000 men enlisted. When the war continued longer than expected, the President called for more volunteers, but few answered. The Union was forced to offer cash bonuses for enlistment and ultimately institute a Draft system.

The first Draft law was enacted on July 17, 1862 and a more comprehensive Draft, called the Enrollment Act was started on March 3, 1863. There were still not enough men to replace those killed, wounded, or captured.

After initially resisting the idea, President Lincoln in his Emancipation Proclamation authorized the army to begin enlisting free Blacks in January of 1863. Later that year he authorized the army to begin enlisting Slaves.

The Union offered $300 compensation to any slaveholders who signed a manumission document freeing the Slave to enlist in the army. The owner also had to sign an Oath of Loyalty to the Union. The following pages are copies of the Bounty Record for the Calvert County. The documents give the Slave's name and the name of the slaveholder who received compensation for the enlistment.

Bounty Records for Calvert County

Name	Company	Owner
Awful, Robert	B	Kent, Daniel
Blake, George H.	C	Mason, John
Braun, John	F	Armiger, John
Braun, Elijah	G	King, James P.
Brawn, Lewis	F	Sloper, James
Bowie, Mason	B	Whales, John
Bowie, William	F	Bookerson, Mrs. George
Brooks, James D.	D	Sedwick, John C.
Brooks, Thomas	H	Hance, Benjamin
Buffelo, William	B	Moulton, Widow
Carter, Richard	B	Clare, Mrs.
Chase, James H.	C	Parker, John C.
Chase, Gustavis	J	Roberts, Richard
Chew, Franklin	G	Moulton, William E.
Chew, William	G	Moulton, William E.
Countee, Samuel	B	Massel, James Jr.
Countee, Lorenzo	J	Sunderland, Betsy
Culley, John	A	Bond, Catharine Duke
Culley, Benjamin	B	Bond, Capt. Duke
Culley, Thomas	H	Wilson, Nathaniel
Dennis, John L.	F	Danton, George
Dorkins, Richard	A	Weems, L.
Dorkins, Virgil	A	Somerville, Charles
Dorkins, William	H	Parran, Benjamin

Dorsey, Philip	A	Stanford, Martha
Edgins, James (Eagin)	D	Sedgwick, John
Eglin, John	B	Moulton, Edward
Evans, Edward	H	Parker, John C.
Foot, Isaac	A	Shedden, William
Freeman, William H.	F	MacDaniel, Dr.
Gumby, James	F	Gant, Virgil
Gant, Daniel	B	Duke, Basil
Graham, James	A	Alnutt, Capt. James
Graham, Richard	C	Alnutt, John
Gross, Everett	B	Turner, Thomas
Gross, Samuel	B	Sedgwick Dr.
Gross, Henry	C	Parran, Benjamin
Gross, John S.	C	Gibbons, Mrs. (Estate)
Gross, Perry	C	Stanford, Widow
Gray, Robert	C	Norfolk, Mary A.
Green, Benjamin	H	Crawford, George R.
Green, John	A	Roberts, Richard
Hansell, Madison	B	Dowell, Benjamin
Hardman, John H.	F	Dalrymple, Wallace
Havens, Elijah	H	Wood, Thomas
Hythe, John H.	B	Kent, Yates
Jacksman, Jacob	K	Blake, Joseph
Johnson, George	D	Sollers, Nathaniel
Johnson, David	A	Allen, Mrs.
Johnson, Major	A	Grant, Richard
Jones, Granger	F	Harrison, William B.
Kerner, William	B	Hutchins, Israel
Macie(Mackall) Joseph	B	Hance, Richard
Mason, John	G	Bond, Duke
Mason, Joseph	H	Bond, B. Duke
Massett, Elais		King, James
Mitchell, John	E	Brown, Sally
Mitchell, Peter	C	Brown, Sophia
Moore, William	H	Crawford, George R.
Moore, George	H	Bond, James A.
Parker, Benjamin	A	Bond, B. Duke

Name		Name
Porter, Alfred	A	Skinner, Levin
Reddly, Alexander	F	Belt, Charles/McCanery, George
Rice, Alexander	B	Hance, Berry
Sawyer, Frederick	F	Talbot, Henry
Scott, George	A	Gibbons, Mrs. William
Sewell, Leonard	A	Young, I.
Shannon, William	C	Glasscer, Mary
Sims, Anthony	D	Wood, Thomas
Steward, John	B	Mills, John S.
Taylor, James	G	Stanford, ?
Thomas, George	J	Plummer, Mrs. Sarah
Wallace, Stephen	B	Parran, John
Wallace, George	H	Gibbons, Robert A.
Waters, Thomas	A	Roberts, Richard
Waters, Edward	K	Boswell, William
Watts, Cesar	B	Wilson, Eveline
Watts, Henry	B	Wilson, Eveline
Wilson, Thomas	H	Sedgewick, John E.
Young, James	C	Hance, Marvin

Camp Stanton, Benedict, Maryland

Camp Stanton was named for President Lincoln's Secretary of War, Edwin Stanton. Almost all the recruits at Camp Stanton were either runaway Slaves or free Blacks from the farms and plantations of the five southern Maryland counties of Anne Arundel, Prince George's, Calvert, Charles, and St. Mary's; and the seven Eastern Shore counties of Kent, Queen Anne's, Caroline, Talbot, Dorchester, Somerset, and Worchester. Wicomico County, Maryland did not exist at that time. Slaves who enlisted on the Eastern Shore were transported by army steamers across the Chesapeake Bay and up the Patuxent River to Benedict.

Runaway Slaves usually enlisted under a different name than their given name. Some did this out fear of being recaptured and other just wanted to replace their Slave name with one of their own choosing.

Training proceeded at Camp Stanton during the winter of 1863-1864. By the spring of 1864, the 7th, 9th, 19th, and 30th regiments of the US Colored Troops had been trained at Camp Stanton. Each regiment consisted of 1,000 men divided into companies of 100 men each. Later, the 4th and 39th regiments also completed training at Camp Stanton.

Slaves and Free Negroes often shared their joys, pains, and hopes at "Camp meetings" or "Bush meetings" Songs were spontaneously created and were called "shouts", "corn ditties", and "spearchils" (spirituals). This tradition continued with the Colored soldiers who trained at Camp Stanton.

The first Battle hymn of Black soldiers was called They Look like Men of War. The song originated among the men of the 9th regiment from Calvert County, MD. General Samuel Armstrong reported he first heard it sung by the 9th regiment during the winter of 1863-1864.

While stationed at Camp Stanton, Armstrong established a school to educate the Black soldiers. At the end of the war, Armstrong founded the Freedman's Bureau. Later, with the help of the American Missionary Association, General Armstrong established the Hampton Normal and Agricultural Institute, now known as Hampton University.

Sources: African American Traditions in Song, Sermon, Tale and Dance by Eileen Southern and Josephine Wright.
Religion, Folksongs of Negroes as Sung on the Plantation, by Thomas Fuller, Hampton Normal and Agricultural Institute

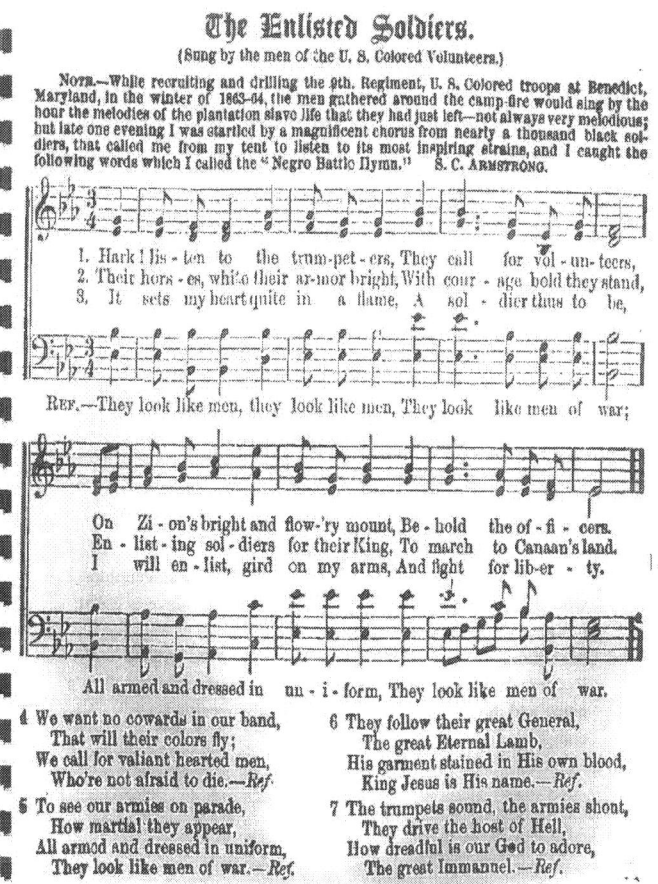

7th Regiment US Colored Troops

Originally organized in Baltimore, in October of 1863, the 7th Regiment, US Colored Troops was transferred to Camp Stanton Benedict, Maryland. In March of 1864, the unit moved to Virginia to support forces defending Portsmouth and Suffolk. The 7th Regiment then went to Jacksonville, Florida and served as pickets and scouts. Picket is a military term for lookout. They engaged in several skirmishes and assisted in building fortifications.

In May of 1864, the 7th fought two battles at Cedar Creek, Florida. The unit moved to South Carolina where they encountered frequent fighting during the 17 day march from Hilton Head, north along the Edisto River. After participating in other raids in Florida, the 7th returned to the James River area and was assigned to the Colored Brigade of the Third Division Tenth Army Corp. There was almost daily combat along the north bank of the James River in late 1864. In the spring of 1864, the 7th took part in the evacuation of Petersburg. After the war the 7th was transferred to Texas.

The following pages are the 7th Regiment Muster Roll for Calvert County. It is interesting to note the number of men who died in Benedict, Maryland prior to the battle, and the number that died in Texas after the war ended.

7th Regiment Muster Roll for Calvert County-Adjutant General's

Name	Age	Rank/Co.	Enlistment		Notes
Bishop, Hicks	35	Pvt G	10/1863	3 years	d. Salisbury NC, P.O.W.
Brown, John	22	Pvt H	10/1863	3 years	
Brector, Thomas	19	Cpl I	10/1863	3 years	
Bond, Columbus	21	Pvt I	10/1864	3 years	
Brown, James E.	22	Pvt I	10/1864	3 years	
Cacine, George	22	Pvt H	10/1863	3 years	
Carter, Elias	21	Pvt H	10/1863	3 years	d.9/29/1864 Ft. Monroe VA-consumption
Clay, Henry	22	Pvt H	10/1863	3 years	d.10/14/1865 Indianola TX-inflammation
Counter, Samuel	24	Pvt H	11/1863	3 years	d.5/21/1865 Jacksonville FL-dysentery
Campbell, William H.	19	Pvt I	10/1863	3 years	
Coats, William	18	Pvt I	10/1863	3 years	
Dorkins, Benjamin	18	Pvt G	10/1863	3 years	
Dorsey, Samuel	21	Pvt G	10/1863	3 years	9/1864 killed in action
Don, William	18	Pvt H	10/1863	3 years	2/10/1865 disch. Philadelphia hospital-wounded
Gross, Matthew	21	Sgt I	10/1863	3 years	
Gross, John H.	21	Pvt I	10/1863	3 years	
Giles, Anthony	22	Pvt I	10/1863	3 years	d.2/29/1865 Pt of Rocks,VA-pneumonia
Gough, Judson	32	Pvt I	10/1863	3 years	d.10/3/1865 Indianola TX-inflammation of bowels
Gray, John	19	Pvt I	10/1863	3 years	d.10/29/1865 Portsmouth VA-rheumatism
Gross, Samuel	25	Pvt I	10/1863	3 years	d.10/10/1865 Indianola TX-cholera
Graham, John	25	Pvt K	10/1863	3 years	
Hicks, Isaac	18	Pvt G	10/1863	3 years	
Hooper, George	35	Pvt G	10/1863	3 years	
Haven, George	20	Pvt G	10/1863	3 years	d.1/15/1865 Salisbury NC-P.O.W.
Haven, Joseph	22	Pvt G	10/1863	3 years	d.9/29/1864 Ft Gilmore VA-killed in action
Hammond, William	20	Pvt G	10/1863	3 years	d.1/3/1864 Benedict MD-typhoid fever
Hone, Anthony	19	Pvt I	10/1863	3 years	
Hin, William	19	Pvt K	11/1863	3 years	
Johnson, Mason	20	Pvt G	10/1863	3 years	d.1/5/1864 Camp Stanton MD-disease
Jones, Abram	20	Pvt I	10/1863	3 years	
Johnson, Aug	21	Pvt I	10/1863	3 years	d.10/20/1864 Portsmouth VA-diarrhea
Johnson, Cornelius	18	Pvt I	10/1863	3 years	d.2/14/1864 Benedict MD-fever
Jones, Richard	19	Pvt K	11/1863	3 years	
Kill, Bazil	30	Cpl G	10/1863	3 years	
Kerl, Peter	19	Cpl G	10/1863	3 years	
King, Edward	25	Pvt G	10/1863	3 years	
Key, Miles	25	Pvt H	10/1863	3 years	d.9/17/1865 Indianola TX-diarrhea
Key, Samuel	19	Pvt I	10/1863	3 years	d.6/18/1864 Jacksonville FL-disability
Livers, Stephen	38	Pvt I	10/1863	3 years	
Mossell, John	22	Pvt H	11/1863	3 years	
Mitchell, Cornelius	24	Pvt K	11/1863	3 years	
Nott, John	18	Pvt G	10/1863	3 years	d.no date, Salisbury NC- P.O.W.
Plater, Aaron	18	Pvt H	10/1863	3 years	
Parker, John	24	Pvt I	10/1863	3 years	
Parran, Henry	34	Pvt I	10/1863	3 years	d.11/27/1863 Benedict MD-chills
Price??, George	27	Cpl I	10/1863	3 years	
Snowden, John	21	Pvt G	10/1863	3 years	
Smith, Emanuel	17	Pvt H	10/1863	3 years	
Stratin, Henry	33	Pvt I	10/1863	3 years	d.7/1865 Indianola TX-bronchitis

Name	Age	Rank	Co.	Date	Term	Notes
Torney, Thomas	25	Cpl	H	10/1863	3 years	d.1/1864 Benedict MD
Ray, John	18	Pvt	H	10/1863	3 years	
Thomas, Richard	19	Cpl	I	10/1863	3 years	
Thomas, Edward	26	Pvt	I	10/1863	3 years	d.6/12/1864 Jacksonville FL-drowned St. John's River
Taylor, Charles	21	Pvt	I	10/1863	3 years	d.1/1866 Indianola TX-cholera
Whittington, John	18	Pvt	H	10/1863	3 years	
Walls, Joseph A.	19	Pvt	G	11/1863	3 years	
Wills, Henry	19	Pvt	G	10/1863	3 years	
Young, General	24	Pvt	-	10/1863		
Young, Daniel	*	Pvt	-	10/1863		

9th Regiment US Colored Troops

The 9th Regiment was formed at Camp Stanton, Benedict, Maryland in November of 1863. They remained at Camp Stanton during the winter engaging in training. In March of 1864, the 9th Regiment went to South Carolina and saw active service under General William Birney. During June, the Regiment saw frequent action in the areas of John's Island. The 9th took part in the Battle of Fussel's Mills and the Siege of Petersburg.

In September of 1864, the 9th Regiment was part of an unsuccessful assault on Fort Gilmar near Richmond. In April of 1865, the Regiment participated in the Union Army's victory march in Richmond. Two months later the 9th Regiment was sent to Texas for garrison duty in Brownsville.

The following pages are the 9th Regiment Muster Roll for Calvert County. Note the number of men who died from disease in Benedict and Texas.

9th Regiment Muster-Out Roll for Calvert County

Surname	Age	Rank/Co.	Occupation	Enlisted	Remarks
Coates, George	21	Pvt/A	farmer	1 Nov 1863	d. 25 Aug 1865 Chronic Diarrhea
Culley, John	18	Pvt/A	farmer	22 Oct 1863	M-out 26 Nov 1866
Dorkins, Richard	18	Pvt/A	farmer	23 Nov 1863	d. 17 Sep 1865 Gunshot wounds, Brown
Dorkins, Virgil	17	Pvt/A	farmer	24 Nov 1865	Prom. Sgt. 14 Aug 1865
Dorsey, Philip	34	Pvt/A	farmer	22 Oct 1863	Killed in Action 16 Aug 1864
Egins, James C.	19	Pvt/A	farmer	22 Oct 1863	M-out 26 Nov 1866
Fooks, Isaac	20	Pvt/A	farmer	20 Oct 1863	d 29 Sep 1865 Browns, TX
Graham, James	19	Pvt/A	farmer	24 Oct 1863	M-out 26 Nov 1866
Green, Benjamin	20	Pvt/A	farmer	1 Nov 1863	M-out 26 Nov 1866
Johnston, Charles	26	Pvt/A	farmer	22 Oct 1863	M-out 26 Nov 1866
Johnston, George	18	Pvt/A	farmer	22 Oct 1863	d 7 Feb 1866 Browns, TX
Johnston, David	20	Pvt/A	farmer	22 Oct 1863	M-out 26 Nov 1866
Mason, John Jr.	19	Pvt/A	farmer	1 Nov 1863	Dischge disabled 15 May 1865
Moore, William	30	Pvt/A	farmer	5 Nov 1863	d 31 Aug 1866 Browns, TX

Name	Age	Rank/Co	Occupation	Enlisted	Notes
Parker, Benjamin	33	Pvt/A	farmer	22 Oct 1863	M-out 26 Nov 1866
Sewell, Leonard	19	Pvt/A	farmer	22 Oct 1863	M-out 26 Nov 1866
Scott, George	18	Pvt/A	farmer	31 Oct 1863	M-out 26 Nov 1866
Waters, Thomas	26	Pvt/A	farmer	25 Oct 1863	Dischge 25 Nov 1866
Green, John	25	Pvt/B	farmer	26 Oct 1863	Dischge Nov 1866
Gross, Everett	24	Pvt/B	farmer	24 Oct 1863	Dischge Nov 1866
Gross, Samuel	19	Pvt/B	farmer	23 Oct 1863	Co. Bugler M-out Nov 1866
Awful, Robert	18	Pvt/B	farmer	4 Nov 1863	d.2 July 1865 Santiago, TX
Brook, James D.	22	Pvt/B	farmer		M-out 26 Nov 1866
Bowie, Mason	21	Pvt/B	farmer		d. 24 Nov 1864, congestive chills
Buffalo, William	24	Pvt/B	farmer		Action: Johns Is., Deep Bottom, Chapin Farm
Carter, Richard	21	Pvt/B	farmer		d. of wounds in VA
Culley, Benjamin	19	Pvt/B	farmer	22 Oct 1863	Dischge Nov 1866 Beaufort, SC
Watts, Caesar	20	Pvt/B	farmer	7 Nov 1863	Dischge OWD Diability
Watts, Henry	22	Pvt/B	farmer	7 Nov 1863	Dischge 27 Feb 1865
Wallace, Stephen	21	Pvt/B	farmer	Oct 1863	Killed in Action 21 Feb 1865, Deep Bottom,
Kelson, Benjamin	15	Pvt/B	farmer	17 Jan 1864	Drummer since enlistment
Mason, Joseph	19	Pvt/C	farmer	18 Oct 1863	Dischge 21 June 1864 Beauford, SC
Mitchell, John H.	18	Pvt/C	boatman	Oct 1863	Dischge disabled 11 Apr 1864 NY
Shannon, William	20	Pvt/C	farmer	Oct 1863	Dischge Baltimore, MD
Graham, Richard	22	Pvt/C	farmer	Oct 1863	
Gross, Henry	23	Pvt/C	farmer	Oct 1863	d. 2 Sep 1866, Cholera, Browns, TX
Gross, John S.	22	Pvt/C	farmer	Oct 1863	d. 2 Sep 1866, Browns, TX
Gross, Perry	17	Pvt/C	farmer	Oct 1863	d. 11 Jan 1864 Typhoid fever
Young, James	24	Pvt/C	farmer	24 Nov 1863	d. 18 Oct 1865 Browns, TX
Blake, George R.	20	Pvt/C	farmer	Oct 1863	Dischge OWD Monroe, VA
Chase, James H.	31	Pvt/C	farmer	Nov 1863	
Hawkins, John H.	25	Pvt/E	laborer	10 Nov 1863	M-out 26 Nov 1866
Mossell, Elias	19	Pvt/E	laborer	13 Nov 1863	d. 18 Jan 1864, Typhoid fever, Benedict, MD
Brown, John	23	Pvt/F	farmer	10 Nov 1863	d. 7 Oct 1864, heart disease
Brown, Lewis	24	Pvt/F	farmer	10 Nov 1863	d. Ft. Monroe, VA
Bowie, William	20	Pvt/F	farmer	20 Nov 1863	d. 6 Mar 1864, Benedict, MD
Dennis, John H.	25	Pvt/F	farmer	16 Nov 1863	Dischge 26 Nov 1866
Sawyer, Frederick	21	Pvt/F	farmer	16 Nov 1863	M-out 26 Nov 1866
Freeman, William H.	24	Pvt/F	farmer	11 Nov 1863	M-out 25 Nov 1866
Gamby, James	30	Pvt/F	farmer	16 Nov 1863	d. 18 Dec 1863, Benedict, MD
Hansell, Madison	28	Pvt/F	farmer	21 Nov 1863	Absent

Brown, Elijah	37 Pvt/G	farmer	16 Nov 1863	d. Benedict, MD
Chew, William H.	19 Pvt/G	farmer	18 Nov 1863	died
Chew, William H.	23 Pvt/G	farmer	18 Nov 1863	Dischge
Skinner, Isaac	21 Pvt/G	farmhand	18 Nov 1863	free
Taylor, James	25 Pvt/G	farmhand	18 Nov 1863	M-out 26 Nov 1866
Mitchel, Peter	19 Sgt/H	boatman	22 Oct 1863	Dischge, Dept. Gulf 26 Nov 1866
Brooks, Thomas	26 Sgt/H	farmer	22 Oct 1863	d. 3 Aug 1864, diarrhea, Beaufort, SC
Moore, George	20 Cpl/H	driver	7 Nov 1863	d. 27 Mar 1864, malaria, Beaufort, SC
Cully, Thomas	18 Pvt/H	farmer	23 Oct 1863	d. 17 June 1864, dropsey, Beaufort, SC
Dorkins, William	21 Pvt/H	farmer	23 Oct 1863	Dischge 22 Nov 1866
Evans, Edward	20 Pvt/H	farmer	22 Nov 1863	Dischge 22 Nov 1866 Dept. Gulf
Gray, Robert	21 Pvt/H	farmer	31 Oct 1863	Killed in action 29 Sep 1864 Chapin Farm, VA
Hardman, John	31 Pvt/H	farmer	28 Oct 1863	Dischge 26 Nov 1866, Dept. Gulf
Wilson, Thomas	25 Pvt/H	carpenter	28 Oct 1863	Dischge disability 25 Mar 1866, Browns, TX
Countell, Lorenzo	21 Pvt/I	farmer	22 Nov 1863	d. 29 Aug 1866, Browns, TX
Price, Matthias	22 Pvt/I	farmer	22 Nov 1863	Dischge 10 Jan 1866
Toadvin, Peter	26 Pvt/I	farmer	22 Nov 1863	d. 29 July 1864, Beaufort, SC
Thomas, George	21 Pvt/I	farmer	26 Nov 1863	d. 12 Oct 1866, New Orleans, LA
Wallace, George H.	24 Pvt/I	farmer	26 Nov 1863	Dischge 21 Mar 1865, wounded
Cuyler, Joseph	28 Pvt/K	mechanic	26 Nov 1863	d. 12 July 1864, Benedict, MD
Hythe, John H.	20 Pvt/K	farmer	26 Nov 1863	Dischge with regiment
Waters, Edward	24 Pvt/K	sailor	26 Nov 1863	Dischge with regiment

19th Regiment US Colored Troops, Maryland

At the end of April, 1864, all the companies of the 19th Regiment came together in Baltimore and began a 100 mile march to the battlefields of Virginia. The unit first marched 30 miles to Washington, DC where they were received by President Lincoln as they passed in front of the Willard Hotel. The march continued another 75 miles to join General Ulysses S. Grant's army of the Potomac at what would become known as the Battle of the Wilderness.

During the next year, the 19th saw action at Spotsylvania, Toloptomy, Cold Harbor, Old Church, Petersburg, Weldon Railroad, Cemetery Hill, Hatcher's Run, Bermuda Hundred, and Richmond.

After the war ended, the 19th service was not over. Like the Colored soldiers in the other regiments, the men of the 19th had enlisted for 3 years. Instead of disbanding the regiment, the Colored troops were sent to Texas to maintain peace and guard the border with Mexico.

The 19th made the trip to Texas by boarding a military steamer in Monroe, Virginia. They sailed down the Atlantic Coast, around the tip of Florida, across the Gulf of Mexico and docking at Brazos de Santiago, Texas. The trip took three weeks and the troops arrived in Texas about June 24, 1865.

The following facts on U.S. Colored Troops was authored by the National Archives:

1. 179,000 Black men (10% of the Union Army) served as soldiers during the Civil war and another 19,000 served in the Navy.
2. Nearly 40,000 Black soldiers died over the course of the war – 30,000 from infections or disease.
3. In 1863, the Confederate Congress threatened to severely punish officers of Black troops and to enslave Black soldiers. As a result, President Lincoln issued General Order 233, threatening reprisal on Confederate Prisoners of War for any mistreatment of Black troops. Although the threat generally restrained the Confederates, Black captives were typically treated more harshly than White captives.
4. Black soldiers were initially paid $10 per month from which $3 was automatically deducted for clothing, resulting in a net pay of $7 per month. In contrast, White soldiers received $13 per month without any deductions for clothing.
5. In June of 1864, Congress granted equal pay to U.S. Colored troops and made the action retroactive. Black soldiers received the same food and supplies as White soldiers and comparable medical treatment.
6. Blacks served in combat as infantry and artillery soldiers. They also performed support functions like cooks, guards, laborers, and scouts.

Coming Home – End of Enlistment

The Colored troops marched to the port town of Brazos de Santiago and boarded the army steamer St. Mary on January 20, 1867. The ship stopped in New Orleans for three days and then continued to Monroe, Virginia, arriving February 4, 1867. There was a two day delay because of ice and then they traveled up the Chesapeake Bay to Baltimore. In Baltimore the soldiers received their final pay and discharge papers. For the first time in their lives, these men were free to go anywhere they wanted.

The battles were not over the for US Colored Troop veterans. They struggled for recognition and had difficulty obtaining their pensions. The US Colored Troops was considered an auxiliary force by the Department of War and therefore not entitled to benefits. The Federal Government did not address this inequality until 1890 and many colored veterans did not receive service and disability pensions until the early 1900's.

Many Colored veterans were denied recognition for achievements and valor. Often recommendations for decorations were filed away and ignored. Another problem for Black and White soldiers was that the government would mail the award certificate and medal to the recipient who would then have to pay the postage due. Some veterans had to return the package for lack of funds.

Most of the surviving Colored soldiers suffered for the rest of their lives from their battlefield wounds or the effects of the malaria, scurvy, chronic dysentery, typhoid fever, rheumatic fever or other illnesses contracted during their service. Regardless of the Colored veterans' appearance, the Black communities in Calvert County were grateful and proud of these men.

CHAPTER IV

Post Freedom Organizations
Secret Societies

The 1790 census listed 8,000 Free Blacks as living in Maryland. Why had these Free Blacks not started their own churches and schools prior to the end of the Civil war? The answer is because of the numerous laws restricting the activities of free Blacks. In 1807, Maryland instituted a policy prohibiting the removal of Free Blacks from other States into Maryland. Any Free Black coming into Maryland could not stay longer than 2 weeks. After two weeks, the person would be subject to a $10 fine per day. If they could not pay the fine, they would be sold into Slavery to cover the cost. After the Slave revolts in Virginia, the penalties became more severe. In 1831, Maryland passed a law which stated that a Free Black coming into the State would be fined $50 for every week he stayed after 10 days. Any person who harbored a Free Blacks would be fined $20 a day after 4 days. A Free Black going out of State should not stay out of State any longer than 30 days without permission. After 30 days they would be deemed a non – resident and subject to the conditions of other Free Blacks entering the State for the first time.

In 1831, all colored persons were forbidden to assemble or attend meetings for religious purposes which were not conducted by a White licensed clergyman or by some other respectable White person. In 1842, a law was enacted that any Free Colored person convicted of becoming or continuing to be a member of any secret society, whether or not it held meetings in Maryland, should be deemed a felon and fined not less than $10. In default of payment, the person would be sold into Slavery for a period of time sufficient to cover the fine. For a second offense, the person would be sold out of State as a Slave for life.

The education of Free Blacks was not forbidden by Maryland law but it was rare to find any group other than the Society of Friends (Quakers) who were willing to teach .Penalties were most severe when abolish literature. A Free Black in possession of such literature was subject to a prison term of 10 to 20 years. Any person aware of a Free Black possessing such literature was subject to a $500 fine and 2 months in jail. In 1857, a Free Black man in Dorchester County Maryland was convicted of possessing "Uncle Tom's Cabin" and given the minimum sentence of 10 years. He was pardoned after 5 years by the Governor on the condition that he leave the State.

Volumes have been written about the sacrifices and victories of the many men and women who have fought for civil rights. While the focus is often on individual leaders and national events, many of our Black ancestors worked quietly in the shadows to create a better future for their descendants. These unsung heroes, working together within the framework of benevolent, masonic, and fraternal societies, made lasting contributions to their local communities, setting the groundwork for- and engaging in- the struggle for civil rights. This section examines the presence, impact, and succession of several such African American societies in Calvert County, Maryland.

The first person to bring this information to Calvert County was Nathaniel (N.M.) Carroll. Carroll was born in 1837 near Smithville in Calvert County. The 1850 census shows him working as a Laborer for the Dowell family in Sunderland. Carroll would later state that he and his brother worked for ten years to buy their father's freedom. In 1857, the entire Carroll family moved to Baltimore city. Nathaniel, now known as N.M., enrolled in the Freedman's school at the historic Sharpe's street church, and would later attend the Seminary school which would become Morgan State College. Carroll would eventually become a Bishop in the AME church, and obtain a Doctorate degree. Dr. Carroll founded or renovated more than 20 churches during his career. Carroll also founded the first old age home for Blacks, which became a model for other homes. His legacy still stands in Baltimore as the N.M. Carroll Manor apartments for seniors.

Dr. Carroll married Caroline Jones of Calvert County and returned there often. During his early return trips, he brought back the message of the Galilean Fishermen. Dr. Carroll was also present at the Sharpe street church in 1865, when Frederick Douglas spoke. Dr. Carroll and Caroline had nine children prior to Caroline's death. Dr. Carroll remarried a teacher from Prince Georges County and had two more children. Prior to his death in the 1930's, Dr. Carroll said the accomplishment which gave him the most pride was the ten years he worked in Calvert County to buy his father's freedom. Calvert County was most grateful for the knowledge of the Galilean Fishermen.

Benevolent societies, or mutual aid societies, have existed within the Black community in America since the mid-1800s. These groups had grandiose names, such as "The Order of The Society of Galilean Fishermen" and "The Grand United Order of Odd Fellows". Each of these groups had a national governing organization with local lodges in many states, including in Calvert County.

The Galilean Fishermen, a benevolent society, was first organized in 1856 in Baltimore City, Maryland. It was founded by civic minded Black men and women. They performed services such as providing for the sick, supporting widows, and paying for funerals. Although the Galilean Fishermen were solely an African American Order, they used symbols borrowed from Scottish Rite Masonry. Galilean Fishermen flourished in and around Baltimore during the Civil War and then quickly expanded after the war, ultimately having lodges in nearly every county in Maryland and Virginia. By 1897, The Galilean Fishermen f claimed to have over 56,000 members meeting in lodges from New England to the Gulf of Mexico. It is not known when the Galilean Fishermen first established a lodge in Calvert County. However, like other lodges within the Order, such as the Annapolis lodge, which opened a school on East Street in 1868, the Calvert County brethren made education a priority. Land records show that in May of 1902, Trustees of Tabernacle No. 47, of the Order of Society of Galilean Fishermen, purchased a tract of land measuring two roods and one perch (1/2 acre and 16 ½ feet). That parcel of land would, in 1921, became the sight of the first Rosenwald School in Calvert County. It would later become Central Industrial School and offer a limited high school curriculum in 1938. One of the Trustees of the "Fishermen" was my mother's grandfather, Charles Stewart, who lived from 1864 to 1957. We can assume the other members were in the same age range.

As the brethren of the Galilean Fisherman aged, their membership declined and the membership of the Grand United Order of Odd Fellows increased. The Odd Fellows started in England and in the 1700s split into two orders, the Independent Order, which became prevalent in the U.S. and the Grand United Order. Despite the popularity of the Independent Order of Odd Fellows among White Americans, Black Americans were denied charters for their own lodges under this branch. Ultimately the "Colored "lodges gained their charters through the Grand United Order in Britain, beginning with the first lodge in New York in 1843. By 1886 the Grand United Order of Odd Fellows had the largest membership of any Black community with medical bills, funeral expenses, and recovering from other catastrophic events like fires.

W. W. CONAWAY, W. E. FLETCHER, C. W. SMITH, Past Grand Masters

Joseph A. Lively, D. D. G. M.
409 N. Mount St., Baltimore, Md.
Telephone Gilmor 6410; South 1910

Joseph F. Chester, D. G. D.
109 Pine Street
Cambridge, Md.

Thomas W. Harris, D. G. T.
24 Fleet Street, Annapolis, Md

Frank B. Butler, D. G. S.
Parole, Md.

WILLIAM T. BRIDDELL, D. G. M.
DISTRICT GRAND LODGE, NO. 14

Grand United Order of Odd Fellows, Jurisdiction of Maryland
Office of District Grand Master: Branch Street, Berlin, Maryland
Telephone 172-W

Berlin, Maryland ....194....

The following pages contain the membership rolls of the Odd Fellows.

Financial Roll - 1945

Dues paid to	No.	Name	J.	F.	M.	A.	M.
Sept 30	37	Howard Bishop	50	50	50	50	50
XXX	38	Wm Thomas	50	50	50	50	50
Nov. 30	39	Wm Smith	50	50	50	50	50
Oct. 31	40	Elias Jones	50	50	50	50	50
[illegible]	41	Elie Long	50	50	50	50	50
Sept 30	42	Richard C. Smith	50	50	50	50	50
XXX	43	Bunting Offer	50	50	50	50	50
	44	Wm Coates	50	50	50	50	50
	45	Henry Jenkins	50	50		50	50
	46	Ben. Hicks	[illegible]	50	50	50	50
	47	Wm Hicks	50	50	50	50	50
	48	Geo. Giles	[illegible]	50	50	50	50
XXX	49	Joshua Giles	50	50	50		
	50	Geo. Emerson	50	50	50	50	50
XXX	51	Wm Emerson	50	50	50	50	50
	52	Benny Simmons	50	50	50	50	50
	53	Ollie Jones	50	50	50	50	50
	54	Clyde Jones	50	50	50	50	50
XXX	55	Julius Harvey	50	50	50	50	50
	56	John S. Tyler	50	50	50	50	50
Nov. 30	57	Earnest Coates,	50	50	50	50	50
XXX	58	Dora Brooks	50	50	50	50	50
[illegible]	59	Irving Brown	50	50	50	50	50
XXX	60	Robt. Brown	50	50	50	50	50
	61	Mervin Jones	50	50	50	50	50
	62	Howard Brown	50	50	50	50	50
	63	David H. Thomas	50	50	50	50	50
XXX	64	Johnny Harris	50	50	50	50	50
	65	Benj Brown			50	50	50
	66	Aron Reid			50	50	50
	67	Raymond Reid			50	50	50
	68	Gross Jones			50	50	50
	69	Clarence Brown			50	50	50
	70	Malcomn Nackall					50

Financial Roll

1946 / 1946

	Name	Jan	Feb	Mar	Apr	May	June	July
1	Howard B. Thomas	50	50	50	50	50	50	50
2	Chas. F. Coats	50						
3	Alex Dare	50	50	50	50	50	50	50
4	Daniel A. Kent							
5	James A. Holland	50	50	50	50	50	50	50
6	Hamilton Chambers	50	50	50	50	50	50	50
7	Henry Kegler		50	50	50	50		
8	David Jones	50	50	50	50	50	50	50
9	Howard Jarman	50	50	50	50	50	50	50
10	Rufus Smith	50	50	50	50	50	50	50
11	J.C. Gray	50	50	50	50	50	50	50
12	Leroy Booth	50	50	50	50	50	50	50
13	Stephen Reid	50	50	50	50	50	50	50
14	George Rice	50	50	50	50	50	25	50
15	Everett Gray	50	50	50	50	50	50	50
16	Washington Carter	50	50	50	50	50	50	50
nov 30 17	James Coats	50	50	50	50	50	50	50
nov 30 18	Chas. Harvey	50	50	50	50	50	50	50
19	Phillip Harris	50	50	50	50	50	10	50
aug 30 20	Henry Thomas							
21	Ashby Rawlings	50	50	50	50	50	50	50
22	James A. Fields	50	50	50	50	50		
23	James O. Gregg	50	50	50	50	50	50	50
nov 30 24	Pinkney Jewell	50	50	50	50	50	50	50
nov 30 25	Nelson Ray	50	50	50	50	50	50	50
26	Grant Wallace	50	50	50	50	50	50	50
27	Joseph Jenkins	50	50	50	50	50	50	50
28	Frank Chambers	50	50	50	50	50	50	50
aug 30 29	Sydney Briggans	50	50	50	50	20		
30	William Brown	50	50	50	50	50	50	50
31	Arthur King	50	50	50	50	50	50	50
nov 30 32	Allen Bell	50	50	50	50	50	50	50
nov 30 33	Lee Leal	50	50	50	50	50	50	50
nov 30 34	Edward Thomas							

		1946	Jan	Feb	Mar	Apr	May	June	July	Aug
Nov 30	37	William Smith				50	50	50	50	50
Nov	38	Elias Jones								50
	39	Elias Long	50	50	50	50	50	50	50	50
	40	Richard C Smith				50	50	50	50	50
	41	Bunting Obbie			50	50	50	50	50	50
	42	William ----	50	50		50	50	50	50	50
Nov 30	43	Henry Jenkins			50	50	50	50	50	50
	44	Benj Hicks	50					50	50	50
	45	William Hicks			50					
	46	Geo Hiles	50			50	50	50	50	50
	47	Joshua Hiles	50							
	48	George Emerson	50		50			50	50	
	49	William Emerson			50	50	50	50	50	50
	50	Benj Simms	50	50	50	50	50	50	50	50
	51	Ollie Jones								
	52	Clyde Jones	50	50	50	50	50	50	50	50
	53	Julian Harvey	50		50	50	50	50	50	50
Nov 30	54	John Tyler	50							
Apr 30	55	Ernest Coats	50	50	50	50	50	50	50	50
	56	Dora Brooks	50	50	50	50	50	50	50	50
Apr 30	57	Ervin Brown	50	50	50	50	50	50	50	50
	58	Robert Brown	50	50	50	50	50	50	50	50
	59	Mervin Jones	50	50	50	50	50	50	50	50
	60	Howard Brown	50	50	50	50	50	50	50	50
	61	David H Thomas	50	50	50	50	50	50	50	50
Nov 30	62	Jenny Harris								
	63	Benj Brown	50	50	50	50	50	50	50	50
	64	Arion Reid	50	50	50	50	50	50	50	50
	65	Raymon Reid	50	50	50	50	50	50	50	50
	66	Ross Jones	50	50	50	50	50	50	50	50
Nov 30	67	Clarence Brown	50	50	50	50	50	50	50	50
	68	Malcomn Mackall	50	50	50	50	50	50	50	50
	69	Isaac Ireland	50	50	50	50	50	50	50	50
	70	Ernest Offer	50	50	50	50	50	50	50	50

Fees for … dues begin Jan 1st

1906

Members dues begin Feb —

		Feb	Mar	Apr	May	Jun	Jul	Aug	Sept	Oct	Nov
73	Benj Brown Jr	50	50	50	50	50	50	50	50	50	50
74	Geo Pratt	50	50	50	50	50	50	50	50	50	50
75	Fred Marcell			50	50	50	50	50	50	50	50
76	Isaac Brown					50	50	50	50		
77	Joshua Hutchins					50	50	50			50
78	Harvey Long										50
79	Bowen Rice							50			
80	Andrew Holland							50	50	50	
81	Oscar Holland							50			50

1947 Financial Roll

#	Name	jan	feb	mar	apr	may	june
1	H. E. Thomas	50	50	50	50	50	50
2	Hampton Chambers	50	50	50	50	50	50
3	Howard Gorman		50	50	50	50	50
4	Henry Jenkins	50	50	50	50	50	50
5	Howard Brown	50	50	50	50	50	50
6	Howard Bishop	50	50	50	50	50	50
7	Harvey Long	50	50	50	50	50	50
8	Henry Kyler		50			50	50
9	James Holland			50	50	50	50
10	Joe E. Gray	50	50	50	50	50	
11	James Coates	50	50		50	50	50
12	Joseph Jenkins	50	50		50	50	50
13	James Kent	50	50		50	50	
14	James O. Booze	50	50	50	50	50	
15	James A. Wills	50	50	50	50		50
16	Rachel Giles	Deceased					
17	Julius Harvey	50	50				
18	Julia Coates	50	50	50	50	50	50
19	Joshua Hutchins	50	50	50	50	50	50
20	James Stepney	50	50	50	50	50	50
21	Joseph Brown	50					
22	David K. Thomas	50	50	50	50	50	50
23	David Jones	50	50	50	50	50	50
24	Dyne Brooks	50	50		50	50	50
25	Guy Pratt	50	50	50	50	50	50
26	George Emmerson	50	50	50	50	50	50
27	George Wiles	50	50	50	50	50	50
28	George Rice	50	50	50	50	50	50
29	Grant Wallace	50	50	50	50	50	50
30	Grose Jones	50	50	50	100	50	50
31	Edith Gray	50	50	50	50	50	50
32	Orrie Brown	50	50	50	50	50	50
34	Edward Thomas	50	50	50	50	50	50
35	Ernest Coates						

1947 Financial Roll

						may	june
	38	Ernest Offer	50	50	50	50	60	60
	39	William Brown	50	50	50	50	50	50
	40	William Contee	50	50	50	50	50	50
	41	Washington Carter	50	50	50	50	50	50
	42	Wilson Ray	50	50	50	50	50	50
	43	William Thomas	50	50	50	50	50	
	44	William Smith	50	50	50	50	50	50
Apr 30	45	William Hicks	50	50	50	50	50	50
	46	William Emmerson	50	50	50	50	50	40
	47	Bunting Offer	50	50	50	50	50	50
Apr 30	48	Benj.						
	50	Benj. Brown	50	50	50	50	60	60
	51	Benj. Brown Jr.	50	50	50	50	50	50
	52	Bowen Rice	50	50	50	50	50	50
	53	Benj. Tyler	50	50	50	50	50	50
	54	Alex Hare	50	50	50	50	50	50
	55	Allan Rice	50	60	50	50	50	50
	56	Arthur Ling	50	50	50	50	50	50
	57	Asbey Rawlings	50	50	50	50	50	50
	58	Aron Reid	50	50	50	50	50	50
	59	Andrew Holland	50	50	50	50	50	50
	60	Richard C. Smith	50	60	50	50	50	50
	61	Rufus Smith	50	50	50	50	50	50
	62	Robert Brown	50	50	50	50	50	50
	63	Raymond Reid	50	50	50	50	50	50
	64	Malcom Mackall	50	50	50	50	50	50
	65	Mervin Jones	50	50	50	50	50	50
	66	Clarence Brown						
	67	Charles Harvey	1.00					
	68	Lucy Booth	50	50	50	50	50	50
	70	Steven Reid	50	50	50	50	50	50
	71	Audrey Wiggins	50	50	50	50	50	50
	72	Philip Hare	50	50	50	50	50	50
	73	Pinkney Sewell	50	50	50	50	50	50

1947 Financial Roll

	jan	feb	mar	apr	may	june	july
76. Isaac Brown	50	50	50	50	50	50	50
77. Oscar Holland	50	50	50	50	50	50	50
78. Charles F. Coates							
79. Clyde Jones	60	60	50	50	60	60	30
80. Ben Simons	50	50	50	50	30	30	30
80. Arty Jones					50	50	50
81. Joseph Hawkins							
82. John Emmerson							
83. Owen Holland							
84. Johny Harris							

1948

	Name	Jan	Feb	Mar	Apr	May	June	July	Aug
1	H. E. Thomas								
2	Howard Gorman								
3	Henry Jenkins								
4	Howard Bishop								
5	Howard Brown								
6	Harvey Long								
7	Hampton Chambers								
8	Henry Kyler								
9	James A. Holland								
10	Joe Gray								
11	James Coats								
12	Joseph Jenkins								
13	James Kent								
14	James A. Borge								
15	James A. Mills								
16	Julius Coats								
17	Julius Harvey								
18	Joshua Hutchens								
19	James Stehney								
20	~~Joseph Brown~~								
21	Joseph Hawkins								
22	~~John Emmett~~								
23	Johny Harris								
24	Guy Pratt								
25	George Emmerson								
26	George Rice								
27	Gross Jones								
28	Grant Wallace								
29	Richard C. Smith								
30	Rufus Smith								
31	Robert Brown								
32	Raymon Reid								
33	David Thomas								
34	~~David Jones~~								

1948

		Jan	Feb	Mar	Apr	May	Jun	Jul
37	Malcomn Mackell			50	50			
38	Mervin Jones							
39	Clarence Brown							
40	Clyde Jones							
42	Charles Harvey							
43	Charles T Coats							
44	Luray Booth							
45	Stephen Reid							
46	Sydney Chiggans							
47	Philip Harris							
48	Pinkney Sewell							
49	Frank Chambers							
50	Fred Morsell							
51	Isaac Brown				50		50	
52	Oscar Holland					50		
53	Alexander Dare							
54	Allen Rice							
55	Arthur King							
56	Ashby Rawlings							
57	Arron Reid							
58	Arby Jones	50	50					
59	Andrew Holland	50	50		50	50	50	
60	William Brown	50	50	50	50	50	50	50
61	William Coutter	50	50			50		
62	William Thomas	50	50	50	50	50		
63	Washington Carter	50	50	50	50			
64	Wilson Ray	50	50	50	50	50	50	50
65	William Smith	50	50	50	50			
66	William Hicks							
67	William Emmerson	50	50	50	50	50	50	
68	Bunting Offer	50	50					
69	Benj Brown Sr	50	50	50	50	50	50	
70	Benj Brown Jr	50	50	50	50	50		50
71	Bowen Rice							
		50	50	50	50	50	50	

1948

		Jan	Feb	Mar	Apr	May	June	July
74	Ervin Brown	50	50	50	50	50	50	50
75	Edward Thomas	50	50	60	50	50	60	50
76	Elias Long	50	50	50	50	60	60	50
77	Elias Jones		50	50	50	50	50	
78	Earnest Offort							
79	Owen Holland	50	50					50
80	Benj Simms	50	50	60	50	50	50	50
					50	50	50	50
					50	50	50	

CHAPTER V
Organizing the Education System

After the Civil War, the Black people of Calvert County changed their focus from freedom to education. There was plenty of work because Whites now had to pay for labor. Money was available to buy land, build houses, build churches, and build schools. The problem was to find teachers. The local Blacks had been denied education during slavery so they could not read or write. It was necessary to go outside the State of Maryland to find Black teachers.

The initial segregated school system in the 1870's consisted of one room school houses scattered through the County. The schools were placed on or near church property to insure they were within walking distance of a Black community. Teachers recruited to work in Calvert County would be provided housing in a community near their assigned school. The one room school houses taught 1st through 7th grade in the same room. The first teachers recruited often had only a 10th or 11th education themselves. Most of the early teachers were female and had to sign a contract not to marry. The organizations did not want to lose a teacher who might leave to start her own family and then more recruiting would have to been done.

Blacks had the opportunity to obtain a higher education in Baltimore, Maryland. Depending upon what part of Calvert County they lived, the distance to Baltimore could be from 40 to 100 miles. Prior to automobiles becoming prevalent, the best way to get to Baltimore was by Ferry boat. People of Color would have to go inside the bottom of the boat with the livestock and cargo being transported to market. The Ferry boat would leave from Calvert and cross the Chesapeake Bay to the Eastern Shore of Maryland before turning back to head into Baltimore. The one way trip would take 12 to 14 hours. A Black student would have to pay to stay in Baltimore if they wanted to get more than a 7th grade education.

It was not uncommon for large Black families to work together to send one or two younger children out of the County to school. The parents and older children would take multiple jobs or give up their share of farm profits to send of the younger children to school. The person receiving these benefits would have to meet at least two requirements. Number one it had to be a male. It was believed that education was wasted on females. The 2nd requirement was that the male be light skinned enough to "pass for white" or some other race. It was believed that the person would have a better opportunity for employment if he left Calvert County and pretended to be something other than Black. This gave mulatto descendants an advantage. This practice was mostly successful. One example was the Bourne family. Lewis Bourne was a Slave and a farmer in Calvert County. In 1859, he married another Slave named Emily. Their first three children were born into slavery. The six younger children were born free. The older children worked so that a younger brother named Ulysses S. Grant Bourne could attend school. He was able to attend Leonard Medical College in Raleigh, North Carolina which later became Shaw University. Dr. Bourne was licensed to practice medicine in Maryland in 1902. He moved to Frederick County, Maryland (initially pretending to be White) and had a successful practice until he retired in 1953, He died in 1956. Dr. Bourne's younger brother James attended Lincoln University in Pennsylvania and became a pharmacist in Atlantic City, New Jersey. Dr. James Bourne died of a heart attack in 1924 when his son James Jr. was only 7. James Jr. would later attend Howard University and became the first Black District Court Judge in Prince George's County Maryland. A wing of the Circuit court in Prince George's County is named for him and the Black Bar Association is name the James Franklyn Bourne Bar Association.

The Black community fought Calvert County for a Black high school starting in the 1880's. Several two and three room school houses were built in the 1920's but they only taught to the 7th grade. In 1927, the Black community tried to embarrass the County into building a High school for Colored students. They combined all the 7th grade graduations at one location. In the 1927 class there were 49 graduates. Five of the graduates were 11 years old, and Ten of the graduates were 12 years old and the rest were between 14 and 17 years old. This display did not convince Calvert County of the need for a Colored High school. Calvert was convinced in 1931 by a man named Albert Cassell.

Albert Cassell was born in 1895 in Towson Maryland. Cassell was educated in Black schools and colleges before becoming a prominent architect and professor at Howard University. In 1931, Cassell purchased 380 acres of water front property on the Calvert County Bay. Cassell's dream was to build a Black community. He wanted to call it Calvert Town and in addition to housing, it would have a casino, hotel, water tower, pier, church, service station, stable , tobacco barn , post office, power plant , bus terminal , board walk, sewage disposal plant and SCHOOLs, both elementary and High school. The funding was available for Cassell's plan via President Roosevelt's "New Deal" initiatives. Calvert County residents panicked. Although White people had the majority of money, land, and all of the government power, they were the minority population. Cassell's project would have brought more Blacks from Depression era Washington D.C. and Baltimore City. The White residents complained to their U.S. Senators who negotiated a plan with the Secretary of interior. They could justify not approving Cassell's plan if Calvert were to build a Colored high school.

Calvert County responded by expanding an existing elementary school in Prince Frederick to an Industrial school. Central Industrial school gave high school diplomas in 1937 and 1938. The first official Black high school was not opened in Calvert County until 1939. The school was named William Sampson Brooks High School. Unfortunately the name was shortened to Brooks High, and the history and legacy of William Sampson Brooks was never taught to the students. The high school exclusively served the Black community of Calvert until the Calvert Schools integrated in 1966.

In 1866, Carroll Church decided to sponsor a promising student. The church chose William Sampson Brooks who was born in Lower Marlboro Calvert County in 1865. Mr. Brooks likely received his initial religious experience at All Saints Episcopal church in Sunderland, because his home was in that Parish. All Saints has a balcony that was used for Slaves and free Blacks as indicated by their baptism records. By 1880, Brooks was living about 20 miles from his place of birth in Prince Fredericktowne. Brooks was working as a live-in-servant for a White family. Brooks' new home was near Carroll Church, an early Black church in Calvert. The Carroll church scholarship allowed Brooks to enter the Seminary Biblical Institute in 1886 which later became Morgan State College.

William Sampson Brooks never returned to Calvert County but remained a powerful influence. The members of Carroll Church followed Brooks' career and would constantly use him as an example of what Blacks could do if only given the opportunity. Brooks graduated with a degree in theology. He began his public career as a pastor of the African Methodist Episcopal Church in Minneapolis, Minn. During his six years in Minneapolis, Pastor Brooks built two churches, St. James and St. Peters. The church would elevate him to Bishop. Bishop Brooks would travel the country and the world. He started other churches in Baltimore, Md., Texas, Massachusetts, and Liberia. Prior to his early death in 1934, Bishop Brooks wrote two books, "What a Black Man Saw in A White Man's Country" and "Footprints of a Black Man."

The one room school houses also had their measure of excitement. In 1937 a Colored elementary school teacher learned that she was making less money than White teachers. Harriet Elizabeth Brown had moved to Calvert for a teaching position after college. Her only family in the area was her sister Regina who had also come to Calvert to teach. Miss. Brown turned to the National Association for the Advancement of Colored People (NAACP) for help. The NAACP sent a young lawyer named Thurgood Marshall to file a petition on her behalf. The petition alleged that Miss Brown received $600 a year, while White teachers in the same category received $1,100 per year. The case was settled in 1939 when the Board of Education agreed to equalize salaries by August of 1939, the date of the next budget in Calvert County. Colored teachers were given a salary increase equal to one third of the differential until the next budget.

    It has been previously noted that a standard clause in female teacher contracts was that they were not to marry. This policy may have saved the county the expense of additional recruiting but it also caused the loss of many talented teachers. For example Mary Winston Jackson came to Calvert County for her first teaching job after graduating from Hampton University in 1942. At the time, Miss Winston taught math at W.S. Brooks High School. The teachers' contract did not allow her to marry so she left after one year. Mary Winston Jackson would later work at NASA and become one of the subjects of the movie "Hidden Figures".

CHAPTER VI
Calvert County's African American World War 1 Heroes

The following individuals from Calvert County died in service during WW1. Their names are inscribed on a memorial in front of the Calvert County Circuit Court house, but they are segregated from the White soldiers.

Alonza Brown

From Olivet. Served with the 371st Infantry, an African - American regiment under French command. Killed in action on September 30, 1918. Awarded the Legion of Honor and the Croix de Guerre from the French Government and the Distinguished Service Medal from the U.S. Army.

James Butler

From Island Creek. Served with Company A of the 808th Pioneer Infantry, an African - American engineering outfit performing construction and demolition duties. Died of lobar pneumonia on September 17, 1918 buried in Oise - Aisne American cemetery, France.

Wallis Curtis

Born in Popular Hill, Prince George's County, later moved to Calvert. Served with company C of the 333rd Labor Battalion of the 20th Engineers. The 33rd was a forestry unit that provided the materials for construction projects as well as wood for fuel, and caskets. Died of typhoid fever and pneumonia on December 10, 1918.

John Gross

From Chaneyville. Served with Company D of the 811th Pioneer Infantry. Died of lobar pneumonia on October 4, 1918 at Camp Dix, New Jersey.

Thornton Gorman

From Plum Point. Assigned to Company 4 of the Training Battalion, 154 Depot Brigade at Camp Meade MD. Died of influenza on October 11, 1918.

Joseph S. Jones

From Parran. Served with Company I of the 372nd Infantry. Re assigned to the French Army's 157th "Red Hand" Infantry. Took part in the Meuse - Argonne, Lorraine and Alsace campaigns that captured nearly 600 prisoners along with needed supplies and ammunition. Killed in action on September 27, 1918 in the Aire Sector. Awarded the Croix de Guerre with Palm.

Benjamin Kent

From Huntingtown. The grandson of a slave, his father moved to Baltimore where Benjamin was born. Benjamin loved visiting his country cousins and moved back to Huntingtown as an adult. Served with company F of the 808th Pioneer Infantry. Died of pneumonia on October 29, 1918 in Meuse - Argonne France.

World War II

The first American Legion Post was started in 1919 by World War 1 Veterans. Discrimination and segregation prevented Black Veterans from joining. The exclusion of Blacks from the American Legion continued after World War II. In 1947, Black veterans in Calvert County chartered their own post. After years of meeting in member's homes, land was donated by Overton and Mary Hawkins to construct a building. Gray-Ray post 220 was constructed in 1955 and named for Norman A. Gray, Jr, and Roosevelt Ray, who were the first two Black soldiers form Calvert County killed in combat during World War II. In 2010, some surviving WWII veterans told their stories. The following pages recollect those stories.

VETERANS
TABLE OF CONTENT

ACKNOWLEDGMENT

LEROY E. BERRY	2
ROBERT M. BOOZE	3
JAMES E. CLAGGETT	4
JOHN W. CLAGGETT	5
GLENWOOD W. FOOTE	7
PHILIP FOOTE	8
MALCOLM G. FREELAND	9
CALVIN L. GORMAN	12
MONROE N. HOLLAND	13
ROBERT JEFFRIES	14
RALPH E. JONES	15
ELMER MACKALL	17
JOHN W. MACKALL	19
CLIFTON R. MORSELL	20
ROLAND A. PLATER SR.	22
EUGENE RAY	24
GENEST REED	25
ERNEST C. REYNOLDS	26
OLIVER W. SHERBERT	28
WALTER WALL	30
HARRY R. WILLIAMS	31

APPENDIX

TEMPORARY CHARTER

The American Legion

NATIONAL HEADQUARTERS, INDIANAPOLIS, IND.

Charter for _____ GRAY JOE _____ Post, Department of _____ MARYLAND _____, No. 220

This is to Certify, that the National Executive Committee of THE AMERICAN LEGION hereby grants a charter to

Earle J. Bourne	Benjamin D. Foote	Malcolm O. Freeland
William H. Gough	Louis H. Khan	Elmer Haskell
James E. Barker	Edward Hastings	Ernest C. Reynolds
William F. Gross	Charles R. Thomas	John H. Stewart
Augustus E. White	John F. Jennings	Cedrick G. White
James A. Clark	Clarence A. White	Benjamin Butler
William M. Chase	Eugene E. Smith	James A. Warren
Julian T. Gray	Albert E. Holland	Roosevelt Jones
Amos J. Daniel		

for the formation of a Post of THE AMERICAN LEGION at _____ CALVERT COUNTY _____, Department of _____ MARYLAND _____, under the name of _____ GRAY JOE _____ Post, Department of _____ MARYLAND _____, No. 220.

This charter is granted on the recommendation of the Department Organization and on the following terms and conditions:

1. All acts heretofore duly and properly taken for the formation of the above named Post are recognized and confirmed by the National Executive Committee.
2. The above named Post shall uphold the declared principles of THE AMERICAN LEGION and shall conform to and abide by the regulations and decisions of the Department Organization and of the National Executive Committee, or other duly constituted national governing body of THE AMERICAN LEGION.
3. This charter is subject to revocation by the National Executive Committee, on the recommendation of the Department Organization, or by such authority that may hereafter be established by the National Convention.

In Witness Whereof, we have hereunto set our hands this Twenty Fifth day of January, 1947.

fourth from left in the second row. (Leroy Berry.)   Berry is pictured standing

LEROY E. BERRY

In 1937, Mr. Leroy Berry was one of the last people to graduate from Central Colored High School in Prince Frederick. As a boy, Mr. Berry would watch the horse and carriage of Sewell Funeral Home go by his house "carrying dead folks" and he thought that might be something be wanted to do. Mr. Berry attended Eckel's College of Embalming in Pennsylvania, and received his degree in 1941. Just as he was starting his career as a funeral director, World War II began.

Mr. Berry entered the army in 1942 at age 23. His college training qualified him to serve as a medic. Mr. Berry spent a great deal of time in Italy and Sicily where he received 3 battle stars. The following is an excerpt from a May, 2009 interview Mr. Berry gave to the Calvert Independent: "I had some close calls. A shell came near me, but it did not go off. That happened to me two other times as well. There were sometimes when things got tight. One time I looked out the window and saw a B-26 Marauder, red hot that had caught fire. You got used to noise. When you heard something like a "whom," you didn't get too concerned, but when you heard 'rat-a-tat-tat,' you better pay attention. We watched the Italians. If they were running, you figured you better run too." Mr. Berry rose to the rank of sergeant and at one time was overseeing a staff of 3,000 at the medic headquarters. He was honorably discharged in 1946.

Mr. Berry married the late Perline Houghton. He has 2 children and 2 stepchildren, 10 grandchildren and great grand-children. Today Mr. Berry at age 92, is the elder pastor at the Church of God in Christ located in Lusby, Maryland.

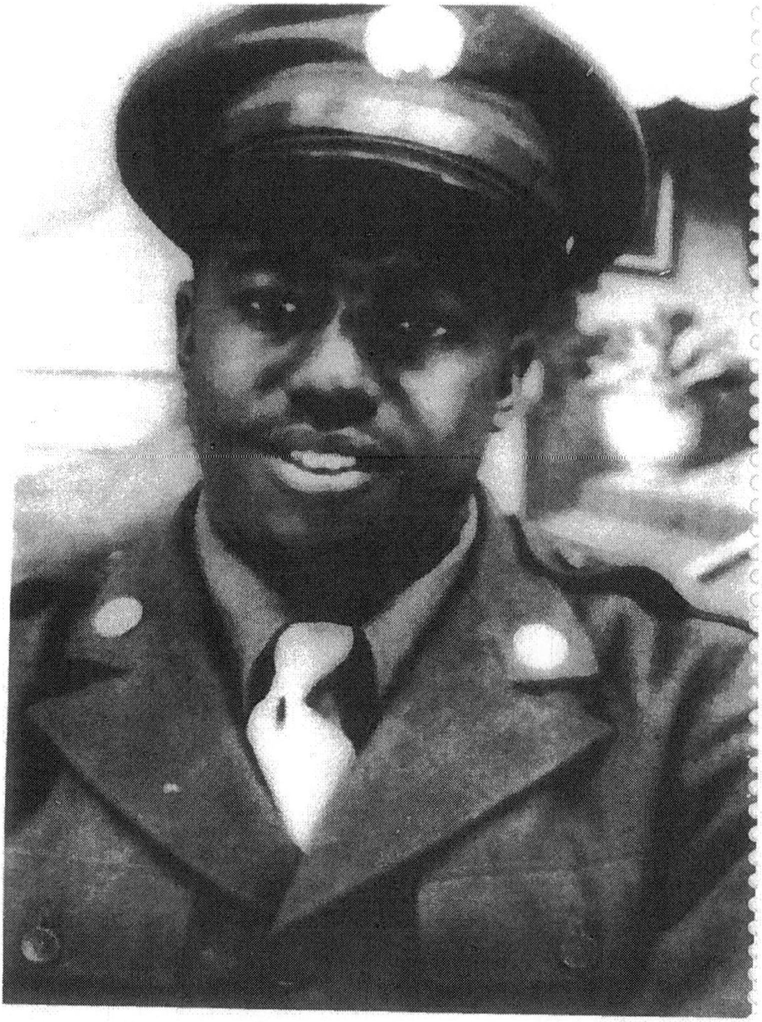

ROBERT M. BOOZE

Nineteen year old Robert Booze was drafted in 1945. Most of the combat had ended, but the training locations remained the same. After indoctrination in Baltimore, Mr. Booze traveled by train to Camp Crowder in Missouri. From Camp Crowder he was sent to Fort Jackson in South Carolina and then Camp Kilmer in New Jersey. From there, Mr. Booze traveled by ship to France. He recalls being sea sick for most of the eight day trip.

After arrival in France, he traveled by truck to Germany where he was assigned to the 3395th quartermaster truck company. His responsibility was to collect abandoned and damaged U.S. vehicles and deliver them to an army station.

There was some interaction with British soldiers and Mr. Booze recalls one Black soldier who was very light skinned trying to "pass" as a British soldier. Unfortunately he could not get the accent right and ended up spending several months in the stockade.

The Black soldiers slept in the barracks which had previously been used by German soldiers. There was frequent contact with German women, which was partly from curiosity but mostly because the Americans had most of the food.

When his 15 months tour of duty ended, Mr. Booze received the Army Occupation Medal along with the World War II Victory Medal. Upon returning to Calvert County, Mr. Booze married Earlene Chamber and today at age 85 he has 4 stepchildren.

JAMES E. CLAGGETT

In 1942, at age 22, Mr. James Claggett was drafted into the U. S. Army. After being indoctrinated at Fort Meade, Maryland, he was sent by train to Camp Forrest in Tullahoma, Tennessee.

Camp Forrest was one of the largest training bases in the country from 1941 to 1946. The camp was named for Confederate General Nathan Bedford Forrest. Possibly for that reason, Black soldiers referred to the base as Camp Patton. General George Patton used the camp and other areas of middle Tennessee as training grounds because the terrain was similar to that in Europe.

After training, Mr. Claggett traveled by troop ship to the Philippine Islands. While in route from the Philippines to Japan, the bomb was dropped on Hiroshima. The troop ships turned away from Japan and headed to the United States.

Prior to his discharge, Corporal Claggett received a Good Conduct Medal, a World War II Victory Ribbon, an American Theatre Ribbon, an Asiatic-Pacific Theatre Ribbon and a Philippine Liberation Ribbon.

Upon returning to Calvert County, Mr. Claggett married Dorothy Reid in 1949 and they raised 7 children who at last count had produced more than 20 grand and great-grandchildren. Mr. Claggett is now 90 years old.

JOHN W. CLAGGETT

U.S. World War II Army Enlistment Records, 1938-1946

Name:	John W Claggett
Birth Year:	1927
Race:	Negro, Citizen (Black)
Nativity State or Country:	Maryland
State of Residence:	Maryland
County or City:	Calvert
Enlistment Date:	16 Jan 1946
Enlistment State:	Maryland
Enlistment City:	Baltimore
Branch:	No branch assignment
Branch Code:	No branch assignment
Grade:	Private
Grade Code:	Private
Term of Enlistment:	Enlistment for the Panama Canal Department
Component:	Regular Army (including Officers, Nurses, Warrant Officers, and Enlisted Men)
Source:	Enlisted Man, Philippine Scout or recall to AD of an enlisted man who had been transferred to the ERC
Education:	1 year of high school
Civil Occupation:	Skilled occupations in manufacture of electrical machinery and accessories, n.e.c.
Marital Status:	Single, with dependents
Height:	00
Weight:	000

Source Information:
National Archives and Records Administration. U.S. World War II Army Enlistment Records, 1938-1946 [database on-line]. Provo, UT, USA: Ancestry.com Operations Inc, 2005.
Original data: Electronic Army Serial Number Merged File, 1938-1946 [Archival Database]; World War II Army Enlistment Records; Records of the National Archives and Records Administration, Record Group 64; National Archives at College Park, College Park, MD.

Description:
This database contains information on about 8.3 million men and women who enlisted in the U.S. Army during World War II. Information contained in this database usually includes: name of enlistee, army serial number, residence (county and state), place of enlistment, enlistment date, grade, army branch, component, term of enlistment, birthplace, year of birth, race and citizenship, height and weight, education, and marital status.

© 2010, The Generations Network, Inc.

While the USO sought to lift morale of all soldiers, it followed the segregationist policies of the military. To accommodate all soldiers, the USO had white service clubs and African American service clubs. It is interesting to note that when the Baltimore *Sun* advertised USO shows in the newspaper, it listed shows for both races in the same article. A *Sun* advertisement for Christmas shows in 1942 read, "...clubs planning special Christmas Eve celebrations are Club Number Four, 128 West Franklin Street, where an open house program starting at 7:30 P.M. will be highlighted by carols, games and other entertainments, and Club Number Five (Negro), 529 Gold street, which will stage 'Night at the County Fair.'"[5]

The USO offered the military men and women activities like dancing, ping-pong, singing, motion pictures, in local clubs in the United States and celebrities all over the world came to entertain or perform for the men and women fighting the war.

---

[5] "USO Pageant Christmas Eve," *Sun*, 21 December 1942, Maryland World War II Records, 1943-1965, MS 2010, Box 162, Maryland Historical Society Library, Baltimore.

UNITED STATES
NAVY
UNITED STATES
MARINE CORPS
UNITED STATES
ARMY
UNITED STATES
AIR FORCE

GLENWOOD W. FOOTE

U.S. World War II Army Enlistment Records, 1938-1946

Name:	Glenwood W Foote
Birth Year:	1927
Race:	Negro, Citizen (Black)
Nativity State or Country:	Maryland
State of Residence:	Maryland
County or City:	Calvert
Enlistment Date:	16 Jan 1946
Enlistment State:	Maryland
Enlistment City:	Baltimore
Branch:	No branch assignment
Branch Code:	No branch assignment
Grade:	Private
Grade Code:	Private
Term of Enlistment:	Enlistment for the duration of the War or other emergency, plus six months, subject to the discretion of the President or otherwise according to law
Component:	Selectees (Enlisted Men)
Source:	Civil Life
Education:	4 years of high school
Marital Status:	Single, without dependents
Height:	00
Weight:	003

Source Information:
National Archives and Records Administration. *U.S. World War II Army Enlistment Records, 1938-1946* [database online]. Provo, UT, USA: Ancestry.com Operations Inc, 2005.
Original data: Electronic Army Serial Number Merged File, 1938-1946 [Archival Database]; World War II Army Enlistment Records; Records of the National Archives and Records Administration, Record Group 64; National Archives at College Park, College Park, MD.

Description:
This database contains information on about 8.3 million men and women who enlisted in the U.S. Army during World War II. Information contained in this database usually includes: name of enlistee, army serial number, residence (county and state), place of enlistment, enlistment date, grade, army branch, component, term of enlistment, birthplace, year of birth, race and citizenship, height and weight, education, and marital status.

PHILIP FOOTE

Mr. Foote was drafted in 1945 at age 18. He was the 4th of 5 brothers to serve in World War II. The 5th brother was Glenwood (see adjoining draft card). The five brothers were inducted before the "Sole Survivor Policy" became law in 1948. That policy was designed to protect members of a family from the draft or from combat duty, if they have already lost family members in military service.

Indoctrination occurred at the armory in Baltimore City, Maryland. Mr. Philip Foote received his basic training as a message center clerk at Fort McClellan near Anniston, Alabama. He received the World War II Victory Medal and the union citation. He re-enlisted after returning to the states.

Mr. Glenwood Foote started closer to home at Fort Belvoir, Virginia, but ended up in Tacoma, Washington (near Seattle). In Washington, Glenwood Foote was trained in drafting (mechanical drawing) because much of the postwar activities involved re-building.

Mr. Philip Foote is a past president of the NAACP, Calvert County Branch.

WWII QUARTERMASTER
Allied & Axis Uniforms & Gear

MALCOLM G. FREELAND

About 2,000 African Americans took part in the landing at Normandy on June 6, 1944, which is known as D-Day. The story of the Black veterans in the Normandy landings has largely been untold. African Americans do not appear in World War II movies such as the "Longest Day" and "Saving Private Ryan."

Malcolm Freeland was one of the brave men who came ashore on D-Day. More than half his company was killed. The majority were killed by landmines because they were the first ones on the beach. Mr. Freeland and the other survivors from his company were re-assigned after the battle. His new job was to transport prisoners of war back from the front lines.

Mr. Freeland had been drafted in 1943 at age 20. After being processed at Camp Lee in Virginia, he was sent to Camp Kilmer in New Jersey to await transport to Europe. Mr. Freeland's Company had a brief stop in Scotland before traveling to England and then by ship to the beaches of Normandy, France. Mr. Freeland was on a ship headed toward the Pacific when the war ended and the ship turned to take them back to the United States. For his service, Mr. Freeland received numerous medals and citations, including the WW II Victory Medal.

Upon being honorably discharged in 1945, Mr. Freeland later married the late Carmel Wagner and he has 1 adopted child and 2 grandchildren. He is currently 87 years old.

CALVIN GORMAN

At age 18, Mr. Gorman was drafted in 1945. Indoctrination occurred at Fort Meade, Maryland where he was placed in the air force. Basic training was at an army airfield in Anniston, Alabama.

Mr. Gorman spent time loading airplane motors in California and in the motor pool in Utah before ending up in Roswell, New Mexico in 1947. In July of 1947 the Roswell UFO incident occurred.

On July 8, 1947, Roswell airfield's public information officer issued a press release stating that a "flying disc" had been recovered from a ranch near Roswell. The alleged recovery of extra-terrestrial debris including corpses has been the subject of controversy since that time. Mr. Gorman left Roswell in December of 1947 to come home to Calvert.

Mr. Gorman married Mary Freeland and today at age 83, he Has 1 daughter, 2 stepchildren, 8 grandchildren and 14 great grandchildren.

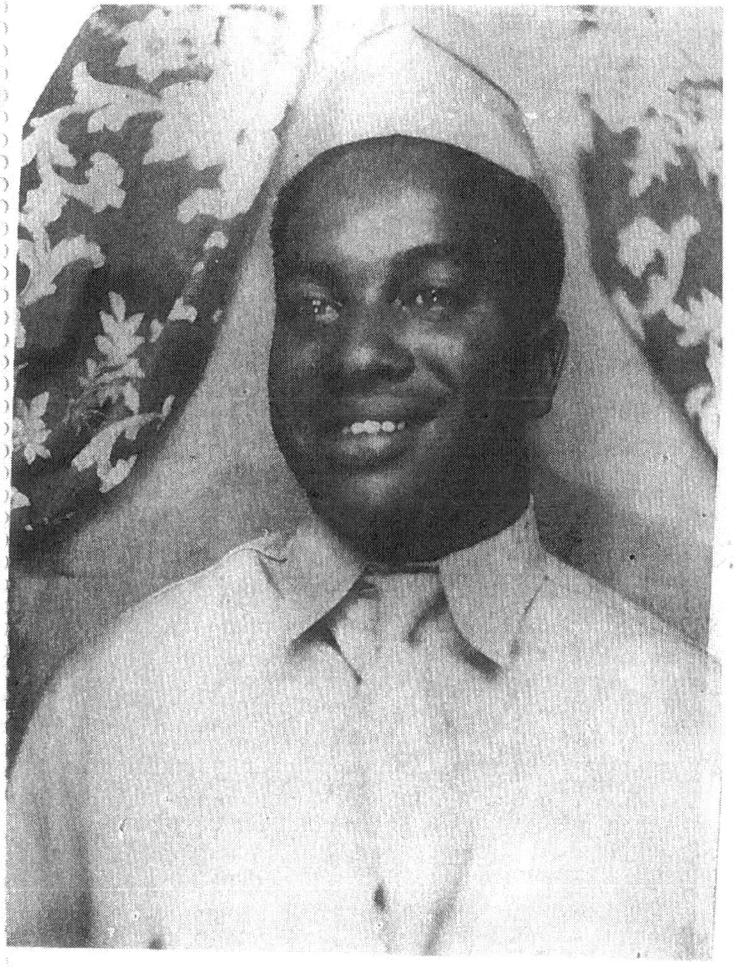

Francis E. Warren Air Force Base (FEW/KFEW)

MONROE N. HOLLAND

Mr. Holland was drafted into the army in 1945 at the age of 19. After indoctrination at the armory in Baltimore City, he was transferred to a number of historic bases.

The first stop for Mr. Holland was basic training at Fort Jackson in South Carolina. There were numerous reports of Black soldiers being mistreated, beaten and even hung by white civilians in the south. Shots were fired at the Black barracks at Fort Jackson.

Upon leaving Fort Jackson, Mr. Holland was sent to Camp Plauche in Louisiana. Camp Plauche was used as a training base, but as the need for troops lessened, the camp was used to house German and Italian prisoners. Nearly half the men at Camp Plauche were Black.

The next stop for Mr. Holland was Fort Francis E. Warren in Wyoming. Before the name change in 1930, the fort was originally called Fort Russell. In 1886 Congress formed four Black regiments, the 9th and 10th Calvary and the 24th and 25th infantry. All but the 25th infantry served at Fort Russell. These soldiers were known as the "Buffalo Soldiers."

During World War II, the now Fort Francis E. Warren trained up to 20,000 Quartermaster Corp soldiers and also contained a prisoner of war camp. PFC Holland drove trucks which transported ammunition to the airfields.

After completing his service, Mr. Holland married Rosalee Fulwood. Today at age 84, he has 6 children, 6 grandchildren, and 4 great grandchildren.

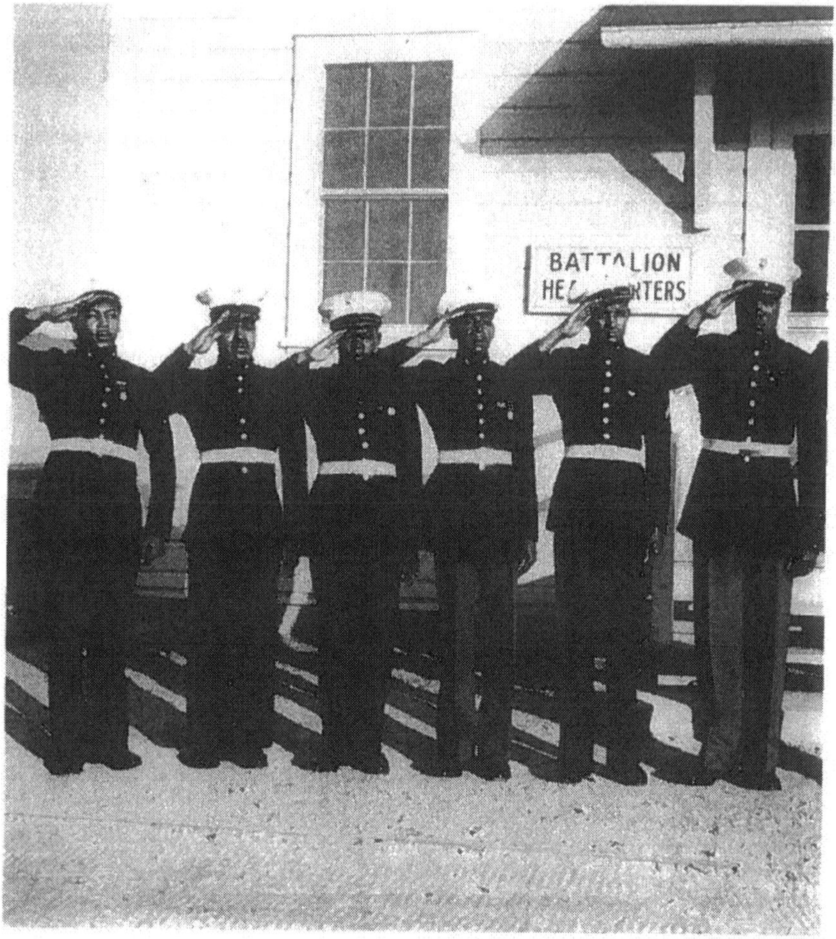
BATTALION

ROBERT JEFFRIES

Mr. Jeffries was drafted just after leaving high school in North Carolina. His first stop in 1945 was Fort Bragg in North Carolina for indoctrination. Mr. Jeffries was then sent to Fort Leonard Wood in Missouri for basic training. After basic training he received specialized training as a supply officer at Fort Francis E. Warren in Wyoming.

While assigned to the 3rd Army, Mr. Jeffries and his company were sent to Nuremburg, Germany as part of the Occupation Army. As a Staff Sergeant, Mr. Jeffries was responsible for supplying 250 men. While in Nuremburg, he was placed on detached duty to the military police who were standing guard a The Nuremburg War Crimes Trials.

Mr. Jeffries received the following ribbons: Good Conduct, European Theatre of Operation Medal, World War II Victory Medal, Army Occupation Medal and the Continental U.S. Service Medal. He was discharged from the army in 1046.

In 1953, Mr. Jeffries accepted a teaching position at William Sampson Brooks High School and moved from North Carolina to Calvert County. He was accompanied by his wife Emma, whom he had married in 1948. They raised 5 children who gave them 7 grandchildren and 7 great grand children. Mr. Jeffries also had a distinguished academic career. Mr. Jeffries moved from teaching at Brooks, to being principal at Mt. Harmony, to joining the Board of Education and ultimately retiring as Supervisor of Secondary Education. He is currently 84 years old.

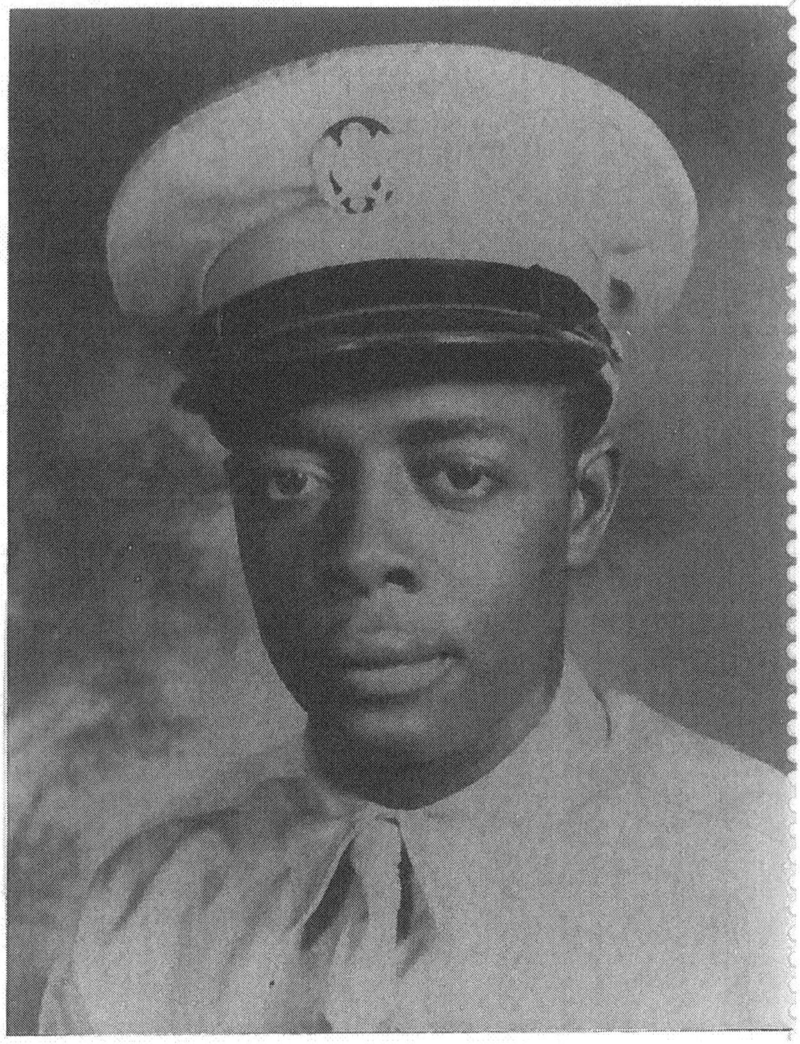

RALPH E. JONES

U.S. World War II Army Enlistment Records, 1938-1946

Name:	Ralph E Jones
Birth Year:	1920
Race:	Negro, Citizen (Black)
Nativity State or Country:	Maryland
State of Residence:	Maryland
County or City:	Calvert
Enlistment Date:	1 Jul 1942
Enlistment State:	Maryland
Enlistment City:	Baltimore
Branch:	Branch Immaterial - Warrant Officers, USA
Branch Code:	Branch Immaterial - Warrant Officers, USA
Grade:	Private
Grade Code:	Private
Term of Enlistment:	Enlistment for the duration of the War or other emergency, plus six months, subject to the discretion of the President or otherwise according to law
Component:	Selectees (Enlisted Men)
Source:	Civil Life
Education:	Grammar school
Civil Occupation:	General farmers
Marital Status:	Single, with dependents
Height:	63
Weight:	129

Source Information:
National Archives and Records Administration. *U.S. World War II Army Enlistment Records, 1938-1946* [database on-line]. Provo, UT, USA: Ancestry.com Operations Inc, 2005.
Original data: Electronic Army Serial Number Merged File, 1938-1946 [Archival Database]; World War II Army Enlistment Records; Records of the National Archives and Records Administration, Record Group 64; National Archives at College Park, College Park, MD.

Description:
This database contains information on about 8.3 million men and women who enlisted in the U.S. Army during World War II. Information contained in this database usually includes: name of enlistee, army serial number, residence (county and state), place of enlistment, enlistment date, grade, army branch, component, term of enlistment, birthplace, year of birth, race and citizenship, height and weight, education, and marital status.

United States Marine Corps

Certificate of Honorable and Satisfactory Service in World War II

This is to Certify that

Elmer Mackall

has satisfactorily completed active service and is this date

Discharged

Entered the United States Marine Corps

16 March, 1944

Began Active Service

17 March, 1944

Upon relief from Active Duty held Rank of

Corporal

given at MPC, Camp Lejeune, N.C.

dated 10 July, 1946

Joseph J. Kelly
Signature

Second Lieutenant, USMCR
Rank

ELMER MACKALL

On June 25, 1941, Franklin D. Roosevelt issued Executive Order 8802 which barred government agencies and federal contractors from refusing employment in industries engaged in defense production on the basis of race, creed, color or national origin. The order required the United States Marine Corp to begin recruiting and drafting African Americans.

One of the first Blacks drafted into the Marine Corp was 18 years old Elmer Mackall. After indoctrination in Baltimore, he was sent by train to Camp Montford Point in North Carolina. The first Black recruits received basic training there. The quota of 1,200 men were housed in prefabricated huts near Jacksonville. Railroad tracks divided white residents from the Black troops, and the Black recruits were not allowed to enter nearby Camp Lejeune unless accompanied by a white marine.

After basic training, Mr. Mackall was sent to Guadalcanal in the South Pacific. The all Black company's job, was to supply ammunition. They slept on the island in one man tents. Mr. Mackall especially remembered the heat and the "plentiful number of snakes."

When the war ended, Corporal Mackall returned to Calvert County and married Lillie Mae Jacks. They raised 6 children who have given them 6 grandchildren and 5 great-grandchildren. Mr. Mackall is currently 85 years old.

JOHN W. MACKALL

U.S. World War II Army Enlistment Records, 1938-1946

Name:	John W MacKall
Birth Year:	1925
Race:	Negro, Citizen (Black)
Nativity State or Country:	Maryland
State of Residence:	Maryland
Enlistment Date:	25 Apr 1944
Enlistment State:	Virginia
Enlistment City:	Camp Lee
Branch:	No branch assignment
Branch Code:	No branch assignment
Grade:	Private
Grade Code:	Private
Term of Enlistment:	Enlistment for the duration of the War or other emergency, plus six months, subject to the discretion of the President or otherwise according to law
Component:	Selectees (Enlisted Men)
Source:	Civil Life
Education:	1 year of college
Civil Occupation:	Farm hands, general farms
Marital Status:	Single, without dependents
Height:	06
Weight:	403

Source Information:
National Archives and Records Administration. *U.S. World War II Army Enlistment Records, 1938-1946* [database online]. Provo, UT, USA: Ancestry.com Operations Inc, 2005.
Original data: Electronic Army Serial Number Merged File, 1938-1946 (Archival Database); World War II Army Enlistment Records; Records of the National Archives and Records Administration, Record Group 64; National Archives at College Park, College Park, MD.

Description:
This database contains information on about 8.3 million men and women who enlisted in the U.S. Army during World War II. Information contained in this database usually includes: name of enlistee, army serial number, residence (county and state), place of enlistment, enlistment date, grade, army branch, component, term of enlistment, birthplace, year of birth, race and citizenship, height and weight, education, and marital status.

CLIFTON R. MORSELL

Branch of military	Air Force
Years of Service; station	1943 to 1946; stationed in Fort Meade, MD; New York; Nevada; Arizona; California; Texas; Mexico; Rome; Italy; France; North Africa; South Africa; Pacific Ocean (Okinawa Island)
Rank; Medals Awarded	Technician Sergeant; 4 medals- Bronze
Enlistment age; current age	Enlisted- age 23; now age 90

Wife (deceased) – Mary E. Morsell
Children – 7 (6 living)   Grandchildren – 12   Great grand children - 21

Army of the United States

Honorable Discharge

This is to certify that

ROLAND A. PLATER, 33 389 230, TECHNICIAN FOURTH GRADE,
COMPANY "B", 78TH SIGNAL BATTALION.

Army of the United States

is hereby Honorably Discharged from the military service of the United States of America.

This certificate is awarded as a testimonial of Honest and Faithful Service to this country.

Given at   SEPARATION CENTER, FORT GEORGE G. MEADE, MARYLAND

Date   17 FEBRUARY 1946.

                           Richard C. O'Connell
                           RICHARD C. O'CONNELL
                           LT COL   AGD

ROLAND A. PLATER SR.

In 1942, 21 year old Roland Plater was drafted and reported for induction in the army. From the induction center in Baltimore, he traveled to Camp Forrest in Tennessee for basic training.

After basic training Mr. Plater received 2 months of specialized training in the Coast Artillery Corp, as a balloon crewman in the Barrage Balloon Program. A barrage balloon is a large balloon tethered with metal cables and used to defend against low-level aircraft attacks. The blimp shaped balloons would be released with the cables hanging down, and the theory was that the cables would collide with the attacking aircraft and either cause damage or a change of course.

The balloons turned out to be impractical because the lines would often break during the frequent coastal storms and trailing cables would short circuit power lines. The program was phased out between 1944 and 1946. As a result, Mr. Plater was transferred to the signal corps.

Mr. Plater was sent to the Philippines where the Battle of Luzon was fought in 1945. The battle resulted in a United States and Filipino victory against the Empire of Japan.

For his service during that time, Sergeant Plater received the Philippine Liberation Ribbon, the Asiatic Pacific Theater Ribbon, the World War II Victory Ribbon, the American Theater Ribbon and a Good Conduct Ribbon.

After his return to Calvert County, Mr. Plater married the late Melinda Brooks. Today, at age 89, Mr. Plater is the father of 7 children and the grandfather of 7 children.

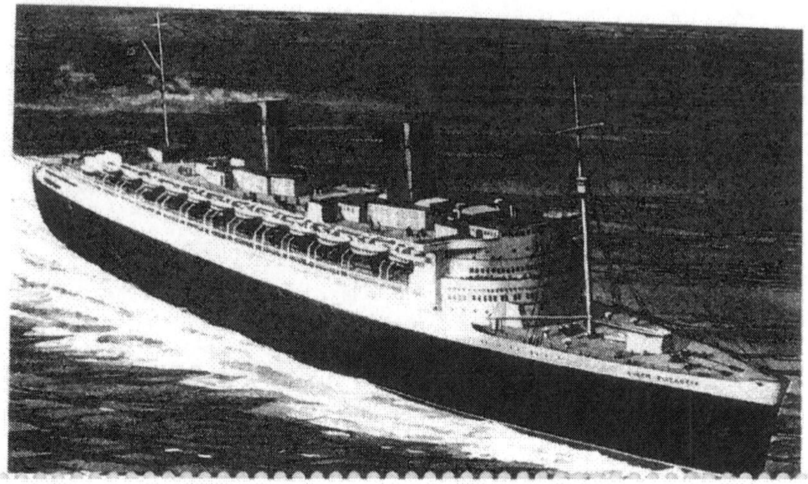

EUGENE RAY

Mr. Ray was born in Calvert County, but moved to Washington, D.C. after leaving school. In 1943 at age 21, Mr. Ray was drafted into the army. After indoctrination at Fort Meade, Maryland, he was sent to an army camp in Georgia for basic training. He received additional Bivouac training in the state of Washington. Bivouac involves mobilizing quickly and setting up tents.

From Washington State, Mr. Ray came back East to Fort Dix, New Jersey. He then sailed on the RMS Queen Elizabeth to England. The first British soldiers Mr. Ray met asked him if it were true that Black people have tails. Mr. Ray's answer was "sure we do."

Mr. Ray worked supplying equipment to the Rhine River in Germany prior to the Battle of the Rhine. After the battle, he helped set up communication in Germany as part of the 29th Signal Corp.

At the end of the war in Europe, the 29th Signal Corp was sent back to the United States, but Mr. Ray was transferred to a trucking division. While with the trucking division, Mr. Ray transported food to the bases in Belgium, South of France and the Philippines. He received numerous ribbons and attained the rank of sergeant.

Upon being discharged in 1946, Mr. Ray briefly returned to the family farm in Calvert before heading west. Eventually, he spent nearly 50 years in Michigan with an auto manufacture before returning to Calvert County in 2003.

Mr. Ray married the late Doris Gagones, and today at age 89, he has one daughter, 3 grand children and 3 great grand children.

GENEST REED

Access to Archival Databases (AAD)

AAD   Series List   Enrollment Results   Partial Records   Full Records

AAD TOOLS   FILE UNIT INFORMATION   Print   Bookmark/Share   Help

Display Full Records

File Unit: Electronic Army Serial Number Merged File, ca. 1938 - 1946 (Enlistment Records)
In the Series: World War II Army Enlistment Records, created 6/1/2002 - 9/30/2002, documenting the period ca. 1938 - 1946. - Record Group 64 (info)

Brief Scope: This series contains records of approximately nine million men and women who enlisted in the United States Army, including the Women's Army Auxiliary Corps.

You may wish to View the FAQs for this series.

Field Title	Value	Meaning
ARMY SERIAL NUMBER	33379689	33379689
NAME	REED#GENEST############	REED#GENEST############
RESIDENCE: STATE	31	MARYLAND
RESIDENCE: COUNTY	009	CALVERT
PLACE OF ENLISTMENT	9375	WHITEFISH MONTANA
DATE OF ENLISTMENT DAY	27	27
DATE OF ENLISTMENT MONTH	10	10
DATE OF ENLISTMENT YEAR	45	45
GRADE: ALPHA DESIGNATION	PFC#	Private First Class
GRADE: CODE	7	Private First Class
BRANCH: ALPHA DESIGNATION	NO#	No branch assignment
BRANCH: CODE	02	No branch assignment
FIELD USE AS DESIRED	#	#
TERM OF ENLISTMENT	1	One year enlistment
LONGEVITY	###	###
SOURCE OF ARMY PERSONNEL	6	Enlisted Man, Philippine Scout or recall to AD of an enlisted man who had been transferred to the ERC
NATIVITY	31	MARYLAND
STATIONED		Fort Meade, MD, Fort Huachuca, Arizona, Manila, Philippine Islands, Okinawa, Ryukyu Islands (South Pacific)
MEDALS		European African Middle Eastern Campaign Medal, World War II Victory Medal

ERNEST C. REYNOLDS

Eighteen year old Ernest Reynolds was drafted into the army in 1943. After indoctrination in Baltimore, he received training at Camp Lee, Virginia before being sent to Fort Devens in Massachusetts.

Fort Devens is the subject of a play based on a true incident involving the confrontation during World War II between Black female soldiers who had been trained as medical technicians and the white colonel at Fort Devens who assigned them to mop floors. The women chose to be court-martialed rather then be humiliated and they received the support of Eleanor Roosevelt.

PFC Reynolds was transferred from Fort Devens and was in England in 1944. Mr. Reynolds worked as a truck driver and transported food in Normandy, Central Europe and Germany. Prior to discharge he received the following ribbons: Good Conduct, WWII Victory, Europe-African-Middle Eastern citations.

Mr. Reynolds married Laura Parker and today at age 85 has eleven children and more than 25 grand and great grandchildren.

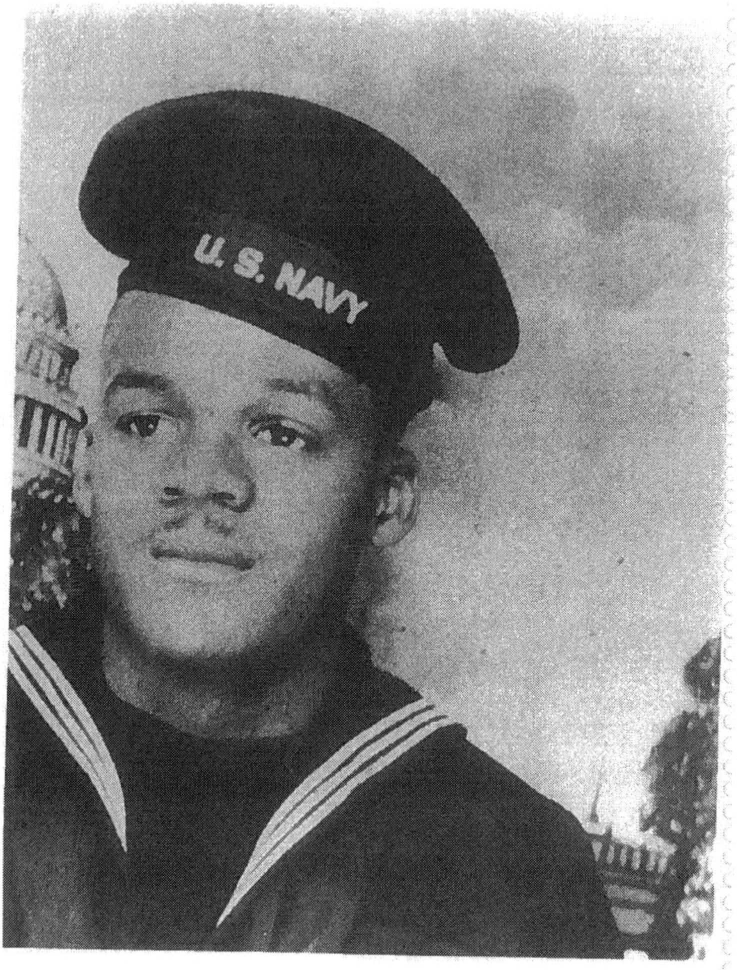
U. S. NAVY

OLIVER WINTERSON SHERBERT
"PETE"

Pete Sherbert was drafted into service in 1943 at age 18. Basic training was conducted at Solomons Island Naval Base in Calvert County. Over 60,000 troops trained at Solomons during the war. Upon entering the service, Mr. Sherbert was asked in which branch of the military he wished to serve. Mr. Sherbert chose the army and was promptly placed in the navy.

Mr. Sherbert first served aboard an LST ship in Guam. LST's were troop transport ships. During World War II troop ships carried thousands of soldiers to and from the United States, Europe, Great Britain, Africa, Asia and Australia. Mr. Sherbert later served aboard a pontoon ship in the Panama Canal. He was honorably discharged in 1946 as a Steward's Master 1st Class.

Upon returning to Calvert County, Mr. Sherbert married the late Hattie Jean Stewart and raised a family of four. Today at 85, Mr. Sherbert has 14 grandchildren and 12 great grandchildren.

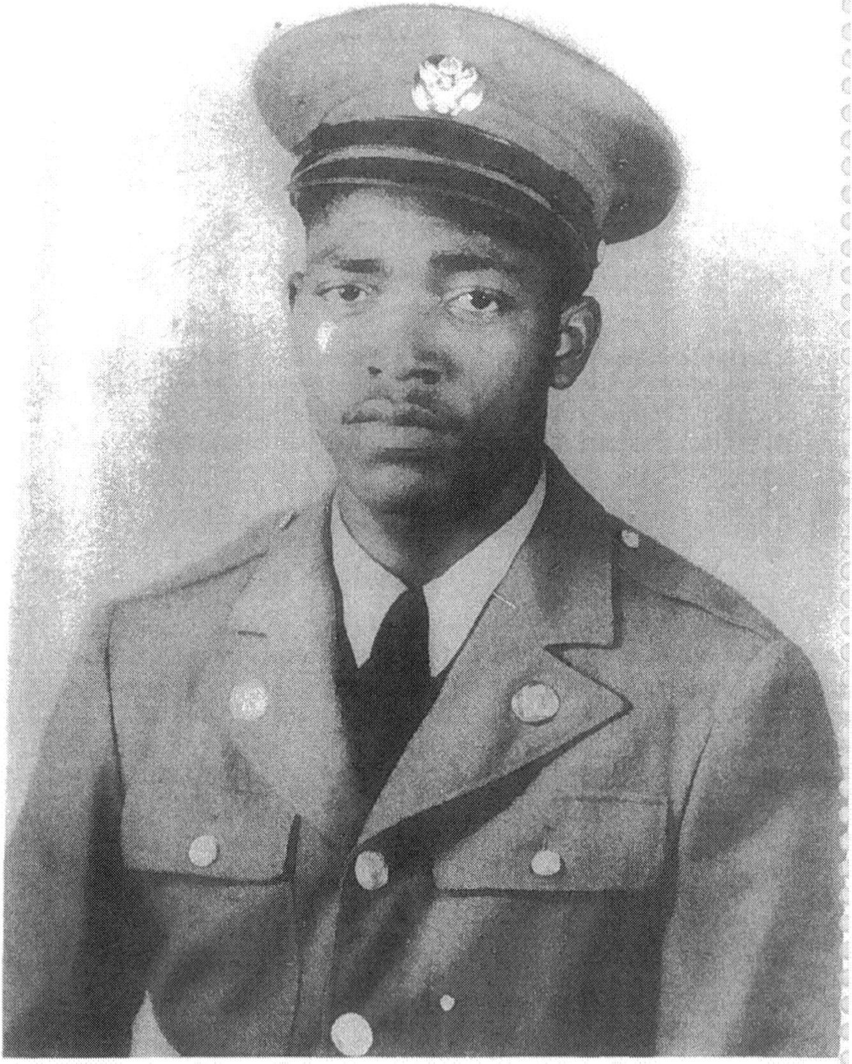

WALTER WALL

Walter Wall was drafted into the U.S. Army in February, 1943. His service time would be short because he developed a hernia during training.

After receiving his enlistment notice, Mr. Wall took Tom Parran's bus to Baltimore for induction. The 20 year old was then put on a military train to Fort Leonard Wood in Missouri. Mr. Wall recalls being covered with dust upon arrival at the fort.

Originally intended to train infantry troops, in 1941, Fort Leonard Wood became an engineer training post. The soldiers referred to it as "Fort Lost in The Woods" because of the fort's remoteness in the Ozark Mountains.

Upon being honorably discharged in September, 1943, Mr. Wall returned to Calvert County and married Thelma Wallace. They have been married for 65 years. Mr. & Mrs. Wall have raised 9 children and have 31 grandchildren and countless great grandchildren.

HARRY R. WILLIAMS

U.S. World War II Army Enlistment Records, 1938-1946

Name:	Harry Williams
Birth Year:	1919
Race:	Negro, Citizen (Black)
Nativity State or Country:	Maryland
State of Residence:	Maryland
Enlistment Date:	27 Aug 1943
Enlistment State:	Pennsylvania
Enlistment City:	Philadelphia
Branch:	No branch assignment
Branch Code:	No branch assignment
Grade:	Private
Grade Code:	Private
Term of Enlistment:	Enlistment for the duration of the War or other emergency, plus six months, subject to the discretion of the President or otherwise according to law
Component:	Selectees (Enlisted Men)
Source:	Civil Life
Education:	Grammar school
Marital Status:	Married
Height:	00
Weight:	000

Source Information:
National Archives and Records Administration. *U.S. World War II Army Enlistment Records, 1938-1946* [database on-line]. Provo, UT, USA: Ancestry.com Operations Inc, 2005.
Original data: Electronic Army Serial Number Merged File, 1938-1946 [Archival Database]; World War II Army Enlistment Records; Records of the National Archives and Records Administration, Record Group 64; National Archives at College Park, College Park, MD.

Description:
This database contains information on about 8.3 million men and women who enlisted in the U.S. Army during World War II. Information contained in this database usually includes: name of enlistee, army serial number, residence (county and state), place of enlistment, enlistment date, grade, army branch, component, term of enlistment, birthplace, year of birth, race and citizenship, height and weight, education, and marital status.

Army of the United States

Honorable Discharge

This is to certify that

HARRY R WILLIAMS 32 751 834 PRIVATE FIRST CLASS
375TH ENGINEERS REGIMENT

Army of the United States

is hereby Honorably Discharged from the military service of the United States of America.

This certificate is awarded as a testimonial of Honest and Faithful Service to this country.

Given at SEPARATION CENTER, FORT DIX NEW JERSEY

Date 3 JANUARY 1946

E. B. NELLIS
MAJOR, INFANTRY

ENLISTED RECORD AND REPORT OF SEPARATION
HONORABLE DISCHARGE

1. LAST NAME – FIRST NAME – MIDDLE INITIAL	WILLIAMS HARRY R
2. ARMY SERIAL NO.	32 751 834
3. GRADE	PFC
4. ARM OR SERVICE	CE
5. COMPONENT	AUS
6. ORGANIZATION	375TH ENGRS REGT
7. DATE OF SEPARATION	3 JAN 46
8. PLACE OF SEPARATION	SEP CTR FT DIX NJ
9. PERMANENT ADDRESS FOR MAILING PURPOSES	215 W 126 ST NYC NY
10. DATE OF BIRTH	23 JAN 22
11. PLACE OF BIRTH	SMYRNA DEL
12. ADDRESS FROM WHICH EMPLOYMENT WILL BE SOUGHT	SEE 9
13. COLOR EYES	BRN
14. COLOR HAIR	BLK
15. HEIGHT	5-6
16. WEIGHT	156 lbs
17. NO. DEPEND.	1
18. RACE	C (Negro)
19. MARITAL STATUS	SINGLE
20. U.S. CITIZEN	YES
21. CIVILIAN OCCUPATION AND NO.	STUDENT X-02

MILITARY HISTORY

22. DATE OF INDUCTION	19 FEB 43
23. DATE OF ENLISTMENT	
24. DATE OF ENTRY INTO ACTIVE SERVICE	27 FEB 43
25. PLACE OF ENTRY INTO SERVICE	CAMDEN NJ
SELECTIVE SERVICE DATA	YES
27. LOCAL S.S. BOARD NO.	1
28. COUNTY AND STATE	KENT CO DEL
29. HOME ADDRESS AT TIME OF ENTRY INTO SERVICE	SEE 9
30. MILITARY OCCUPATIONAL SPECIALTY AND NO.	MED TECH 409
31. MILITARY QUALIFICATION AND DATE	NONE

32. BATTLES AND CAMPAIGNS
CENTRAL EUROPE   NORTHERN FRANCE   RHINELAND   GO 33 WD 45 AS AMENDED

33. DECORATIONS AND CITATIONS
ASIATIC PACIFIC SERVICE MEDAL   EUROPEAN AFRICAN MIDDLE EASTERN SERVICE MEDAL   GOOD CONDUCT MEDAL   WORLD WAR II VICTORY MEDAL

34. WOUNDS RECEIVED IN ACTION
NONE

35. LATEST IMMUNIZATION DATES
SMALLPOX 6 JUL 45   TYPHOID 6 MAR 44   TETANUS 27 FEB 43   OTHER TY 14 JUL 45

36. SERVICE OUTSIDE CONTINENTAL U.S. AND RETURN

DATE OF DEPARTURE	DESTINATION	DATE OF ARRIVAL
26 NOV 43	ETO	4 DEC 43
25 JUL 45	WPTO	31 AUG 45
30 NOV 45	USA	20 DEC 45

37. TOTAL LENGTH OF SERVICE
CONTINENTAL SERVICE: 0 YEARS 9 MONTHS 12 DAYS
FOREIGN SERVICE: 2 YEARS 0 MONTHS 25 DAYS

38. HIGHEST GRADE HELD: PFC

39. PRIOR SERVICE: NONE

40. REASON AND AUTHORITY FOR SEPARATION
CONVENIENCE OF THE GOVT AR 615-365 15 DEC 44 & RR1-1 DEMOBILIZATION

41. SERVICE SCHOOLS ATTENDED: NONE

42. EDUCATION (Years): Grammar 8   High School 4   College 2½

PAY DATA

43. LONGEVITY FOR PAY PURPOSES	2 YEARS 10 MONTHS 9 DAYS
44. MUSTERING OUT PAY – TOTAL	$300 THIS PAYMENT $100
45. SOLDIER DEPOSITS	NONE
46. TRAVEL PAY	$6.45
47. TOTAL AMOUNT, NAME OF DISBURSING OFFICER	$118.85 J HARRIS COL FD

INSURANCE NOTICE

IMPORTANT   IF PREMIUM IS NOT PAID WHEN DUE OR WITHIN THIRTY-ONE DAYS THEREAFTER, INSURANCE WILL LAPSE. MAKE CHECKS OR MONEY ORDERS PAYABLE TO THE TREASURER OF THE U. S. AND FORWARD TO COLLECTIONS SUBDIVISION, VETERANS ADMINISTRATION, WASHINGTON 25, D.C.

48. KIND OF INSURANCE	49. HOW PAID	50. Effective Date of Allotment Discontinuance	51. Date of Next Premium Due (One month after 50)	52. PREMIUM DUE EACH MONTH	53. INTENTION OF VETERAN TO Continue / Discontinue
NSLI X	U.S. Govt X, Direct to V.A. X	31 DEC 45	31 JAN 46	$6.50	Continue X

54. (Right thumb print)

55. REMARKS
LAPEL BUTTON ISSUED
INACTIVE ERC FROM 19 FEB 43 TO 26 FEB 43
ASR SCORE (2 SEP 45) 60

56. SIGNATURE OF PERSON BEING SEPARATED: Harry Williams

57. PERSONNEL OFFICER
J E WHITE JR
CAPT AC

WD AGO FORM 53-
1 November 1944

This form supersedes all previous editions of WD AGO Forms 53 and 55 for enlisted persons entitled to an Honorable Discharge, which will not be used after receipt of this revision.

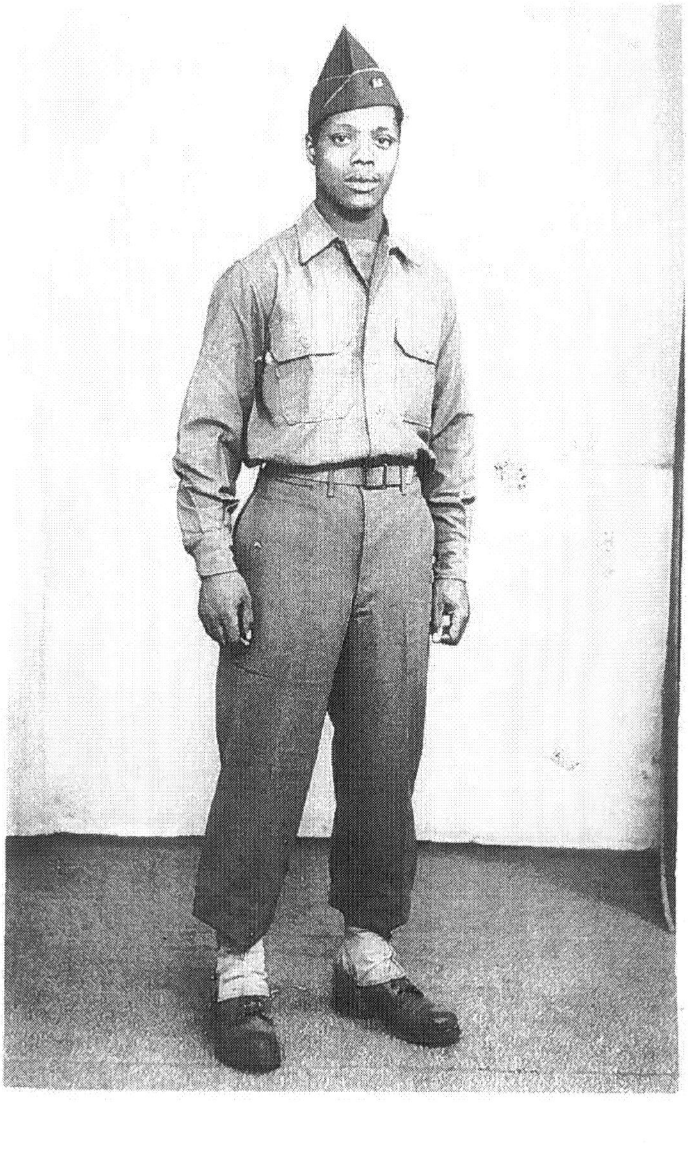

CHAPTER VII
Legacy

The Black community in Calvert County had tremendous obstacles to overcome. Blacks did not always have to work alone. Many White people often assisted. White abolitionist helped runaways from the very beginning of Slavery. Whites helped Blacks to learn to read and write. There were times that White's risked their own lives for Blacks. An example is the Rand case in 1908. Arthur Rand, also known as John Jones was a Black man accused of robbing and assaulting a White women. Rand was brought to the woman's home near Mt. Harmony for a preliminary hearing. Upon finding enough evidence to hold Rand for trial, Justice Bowen ordered Sheriff Mead to take him to jail. By this time, word had spread and a mob had gathered to lynch Rand. Justice Bowen and Sheriff Mead speed away in a carriage with the defendant and the mob chasing. Instead of going to the jail, Bowen and Mead abandoned the carriage and took the defendant 10 miles by foot to the train station. They were able to get him safely to Baltimore to await trial. When Rand returned for trial several months later, the mob had cooled because several White men had testified that the alleged victim did not have a good reputation.
Rand was still sentenced by Circuit judge Briscoe to 21 years for the assault and 10 years for stealing a $40 check and another 4 years for stealing a horse. On the same day, Judge Briscoe sentenced another Black man to 3 years in prison for stealing $3.00. Rand and the other man were handcuffed together on the train ride to the prison in Baltimore and both stated they were just happy to be out of Calvert County.

The Civil rights era came slowly to Calvert County. Schools did not fully integrate until 1966. The library and other public buildings were off limits to Blacks. In the 1950's the Director of the public library defended segregation by claiming that "Colored people have venereal diseases which can be spread thru books". There was not a lot of effort put into solving crimes against Blacks and even when the perpetrator was caught the punishments were light. In 1952, two young Black males were found dead on the side of the road. Their heads had been bashed and the bodies stacked on top of each other to form the shape of a cross. Law enforcement stated the case would either be solved shortly or never. The correct answer was never. Two people were convicted of killing other Blacks during that 1952 year and were sentenced to only 4 years.

CHAPTER VIII
Calvert County's African-American Heritage
(Past and Present)
The purpose of this chapter is to document the contributions African-Americans in Calvert County have made to the County infra-structure. The majority of buildings created by African-Americans, that still exist, are churches. Every church is not referenced but, hopefully, every denomination is represented. Several school buildings have survived but are used for other purposes (See the "To learn more" section). Working the water and farming were traditional ways for African- Americans to make a living in Calvert County, but this chapter also shows numerous buildings designed to provide services and entertainment. This chapter attempts to accurately portray the time periods discussed and at times may refer to African- Americans as Black or Colored.

Dunkirk
Peter's UMC – 2785 Chaney Road
The current building dates from 1909. There has been a church on the site since 1857.

Owings
Paris Center (pictured) – Rt. 260 Owings - The Paris Center was constructed by Alvin Hurley Jr. (circa 1980)

Gray's Field – 2962 Fowler Road (North side)
This site was the home of the Owings Eagles, a Negro Minor League Baseball team, from the 1930's to 1997. The players' love of the game is exemplified in the career of George H. Spriggs (pictured). Born in 1941, George played for the Eagles from 1953 – 1958. He made it to the major leagues in 1971 at age 30.

Reid Building – 7995 Old Solomon's Island Road
Named for the first owner, Nick Reid, this building site served the Black community as a pool hall and bar in the 1960's and the early 1970's. The current building was constructed and owned by Sherman and Mabel Smith.

Side Routes of Interest
Cooper's UMC – 9370 Southern Maryland Boulevard This church has served the Calvert community since 1914 and the cemetery is an excellent resource for genealogy research.
Fairview Library – 8120 Southern Maryland Boulevard
This library is an excellent resource center for African American History and is also the site of Calvert County tourism information.

Sunderland
H. Elizabeth Brown – 100 Pushaw Station Road (Roadside Marker)
Harriet Elizabeth Brown successfully sued the Calvert County Board of Education for equal pay for African American teachers in 1937. Salaries were equalized across the state as a result. The case was citedacross the nation. Thurgood Marshall was Miss Brown's attorney for this landmark case.

Clyde Jones Road – Windy Willow Farm
Clyde Jones sharecropped with his father until 1926, when he and his wife, Pearl, moved to Washington, D.C. and worked and saved enough to buy 25 acres on which to erect a sawmill. The saw mill has long since been demolished but the farm remains.

Complete history at the Calvert County Historical Society (CCHS)

Mt. Hope UMC – Route 2 and Dalrymple Road
Originally built in 1860, it is listed on the Maryland Historic Site Inventory.

Side route of interest
JT's Kitchen – 36 Dalrymple Road
Rest stop which provides freshly made soul food. Owned and operated by a local African-American businessman.

Chesapeake Beach
St. Edmond's UMC – 3000 Dalrymple Road
St. Edmond's has served the African-American community as a church and school since 1867.

Christiana Parran (pictured) – corner of Dalrymple Road and Christiana Parran Road

The road is named in honor of an African-American business woman. Parran ran a post office and store. She acquired land and wealth. Parran died in 1940 and is buried at St. Edmond's church.

Huntingtown

Reid School Buses—Ponds Wood Road
Most of the Calvert County bus contractors are African American. The Reid family bus business started in 1938 and they are in their 4th generation. ++See History of School bus contractor since 1923 at the Calvert County Historical Society.

The Ponds Wood Road community is an example of the transition from tenant farming to land ownership by African Americans prior to 1950. The road is lined with homes of descendants of first time landowners from that period. It is listed on the Maryland Historic site inventory.

Discount Liquors/Gas Stop – 5005 Solomon's Island Road Formerly Kyler's Store and the Burris Club. This building served the Black community as a pool hall and
Bar in the 1960's and the early 70's. The building exterior remains unchanged.

Side route of interest
Bethel Way of the Cross church Cherry Hill Road - Large African American Church.

ODD Fellows Hall/ Masonic Lodge – 10 Sheckell's Road
The Colored Odd Fellows in the 40's and 50's helped their members and the community at times of sickness or death.

Bowen's Groceries – 4300 Hunting Creek Road
Formerly "Mogck"s store, has served the Black and White community since the 1930's. The store extended credit to Blacks when most stores would not.

Danigus Lane off Kings Landing Road
Named for Daniel and Augusta (Gussie) Kent. The surrounding property on Kings Landing Road was first owned by James P. King. In 1837, King purchased a slave named Susan from the estate of Maryland Governor, Joseph Kent (born in Lower Marlboro, Calvert County). King fathered three children by Susan, who became a free landowner by 1850. Susan's mulatto son, Benjamin, born in 1839 acquired 80 more acres after marrying Rachel in 1870. Benjamin's son, Daniel, added another 250 acres after marrying Gussie in 1911, and their son Gayhart added another 125 acres in 1950 after marrying Viola. (Complete history at the Calvert Historical Society).

Kings Landing Park – end of Kings Landing Road
This park was privately owned until 1950 when acquired by the YMCA of Baltimore and named Camp Mohawk. The camp served Negro children during segregation, many of whom came from the Washington and Baltimore areas. (Complete History at the Calvert Historical Society).

Side Route of interest
Smokey Road, Huntingtown Road to Mill Branch Road or Lower Marlboro Road to Huntingtown Road to Mill Branch Road Arthur Carter appeared in the 1870 census of Calvert at age 14 living with an unrelated family. After marrying Priscilla, they had a son Robert, who married August (Gussie). Their descendants are on both sides of Smokey Road. A complete history and genealogy is at the Calvert Historical Society. Their history includes the Ray, Freeland and Kent families.

Youngs UMC – Huntingtown Creek and Bowie Shop Road Youngs was built by Blacks in 1898 as part of the four circuit of churches, including Huntingtown, Patuxent and Plum Point. The building structure has not changed.

Hi Hat Club – 3615 Solomon's Island Road
(no longer exists) Opened in 1946, this beer tavern became a popular gathering place for Blacks by booking entertainers from Baltimore and Washington. The club closed in the early 1960's.

Locks Store – ¼ mile north of Hi Hat Club around 3615 Solomon's Island Road (no longer exists)

The store featured one of the first gas pumps in Calvert County.

Kingdom Hall 3750 Solomons Island Road. Jehovah's Witness Faith.

Carroll Victoria Building – 3720 Solomon's Island Road
Masonic Lodge and NAACP meeting place.

Leroy Berry home/Mortuary (pictured is an advertisement from 1970) 3690 Solomon's Island Road
Mr. Berry was a decorated WWII veteran who also was one of the Calvert's first Black morticians and school bus contractors. The mortuary can still be seen behind the house.

Graduate Funeral Director
and Embalmer
LEROY E. BERRY
Huntingtown, Md. 20639
Phone: Area Code 301 535-9474
Satisfactory Funeral Service

Patuxent UM – 3500 Solomons Island Road
Built in 1883 and rebuilt in 1896, this historic church housed the congregation of worshipers that formed between 1875 and 1880. Though the church was destroyed by fire in 1893, within 7 months, the present structure was erected on the site.

Side Route of interest
Plum Point UMC – 1800 Stinnett Road
The original "Plum Point Chapel" was built between 1789 and 1810. The Blacks who attended the chapel were usually house servants and wet nurses for their slave masters and sat in the balconies. The building was later purchased by the Colored congregation.

Complete history at Calvert County Historical Society (CCHS).

Prince Frederick

The County seat for Calvert County. In 1957 Calvert was home for 6,972 whites and 5,128 Colored citizens. It was estimated that 350 colored citizens lived in the
Prince Frederick area.
Southern Maryland Islamic Center – Route 4 – This mosque has existed since the 1980's.

Dares Beach Road (East)

Mt. Olive UMC – 811 Dares Beach Road, African- American congregation since the early 1900's.

William Sampson Brooks High School– 1305 Dares Beach Road –Served the community as the only Colored high school during segregation.

Sewells Funeral Home – 1451 Dares Beach Road –
Family owned and operated since 1938. It is an excellent resource for genealogy research.

Wallville School (Pictured) 1301 Dares Beach Road
The original school has very recently been moved to this site and has been renovated. A historic marker highlights the background of this school which served the African-American community from the 1880's until 1934. (see "To learn more section" for details of all one room school houses).

Morning Star Tabernacle No. 47, Order of the Society of Galilean Fisherman adjacent to old Central Industrial School circa 1905. Benevolent African American Fraternal organization assisted members who needed funds for illnesses or funeral expenses. One of the rules of the society required all members to renounce their right to apply for protection or redress against each other to the civil law, and to bring all their grievances to their lodge for settlement by a court of inquiry, under penalty of expulsion.

Built in 1921 as a Rosenwald School. Became Central Elementary and then Central Industrial School and offered a High School curriculum.

Old Prince Frederick

Calvert County Circuit Court – 175 Main Street
Contains land and marriage records which are available for genealogical research and review.

Evans Hotel– No longer standing; used to be across from the courthouse on Duke Street. The first level of the building served Whites and the basement, known as "Sachs" served Colored.

Calvert County Historical Society (CCHS) – 70 Church Street
Located at the historic Linden Hall, it serves as a Resource Center for African-American History and genealogy.

Prince Frederick – Route 231
Stewart Family Home – 1115 Hallowing Point Road
This historic house was built in 1929 at request of original owner, John Stewart, a Black man, who owned the oyster house next door. One of the first homes with in-door plumbing, the family housed new Black teachers that came to the County. At one point armed guards were posted around the home because of threats by Whites who wanted to burn the house down.

Melvin's Place – 1155 Hallowing Point Road Formerly Stewart's oyster house, then Stewart's Bar and Duke's Bar, and finally Melvin's (still a family owned business). Since the 1920's the building has served the Black community as a bar, store, movie theatre, carnival, barber shop motorcycle club, and Tavern.

Carroll Western Cemetery – Barstow Road off 231 Formerly Carroll Church and school. Wilson Mason, one of the first Black undertakers is buried here. Mason Road off rt. 231 was named for his family. Side Route of interest Carroll Western Church 2325 Adelina Road

The Black congregations of Carroll and Western Churches merged in the 1950's. Western Church had existed since 1895 according to Calvert County land records.

Seagull Beach – Seagull Beach Road (off 231) now a private community.

Seagull Beach was a segregated Colored beach from the late 1950's to 1970. It was part of the "Chitlin' Circuit." Entertainers were backed by the house band "The Hounds".

Prince Frederick
Harris House – 1930 Joe Harris Road
This two-story colonial was formerly a slave owner's house. Remnants of slave cabins are at the rear of the property.
Biscoe-Gray Heritage Farm – 2695 Grays Road
The Biscoe-Gray Heritage Farm is a site rich in natural and cultural resources. It is a living laboratory to explore, understand, and experience Calvert County agricultural practices and life styles.

John Rice Forge and House (pictured) – Grays Road Rice was an African American Blacksmith.

Greater Bible Way Church – 2300 Sixes Road
This is one of the larger African American churches. It was built in 1952.

Brown's Church – Parker's Creek Road
This edifice was part of the circuit that included Mt. Olive, Carroll and Western Churches. To get to church dedicated members used to row up or down the Bay, then walk up to the church. Records indicate it was dedicated in 1898 and closed in 1972. The cemetery remains in use.

Port Republic / Island Creek
Brother's Johnson Complex – 1925 Laveille Road
This sizable farm complex is owned by descendants of Civil War Veteran, Albert Gantt. Texas Longhorn cattle can be seen grazing in the pastures.

Harold Parker House – Williams Wharf Road
This historic residence was built by former slaves during the 1860's or 1870's.

Bourne House (pictured) – Ben Creek Road Louis Bourne, a former slave, who was owned by a doctor, resided here. One of his sons, Ulysses S. Grant Bourne, became the first Black doctor from Calvert County in 1903. Another son born in this house was James Franklyn Bourne, also a doctor and father of James Franklyn Bourne, Jr, who became the first Black District Court Judge in Montgomery County and forwhom the Bourne wing of the Circuit Court in Prince George's County is named.

Emmanuel Seventh Day Adventist church – 105 Kingsberry Court, St. Leonard

St. Leonard
Brooks UMC – 5550 Mackall Road
One of the oldest African American churches in Calvert County, dating back to 1867.

Jefferson Patterson Park – 10515 Mackall Road
At this site, Morgan State University Marine research facility is working with the Watermen's Association. Also this is the site of Sukeet's Slave cabin.
Interesting Side Trip
Norman Gray House – St. Leonard Road
Built by African American, Norman Gray in 1919, this home continues to stand today.

Lusby

Smith's Store – 9470 H.G. Trueman Road North Smith, a Black woman owned this store from the 1950's to 1963. The family members were also school bus contractors.

See history at Calvert County Historical Society.

Thomas Foote House – Coster Road Owned by an affluent Black family in 1800's.

Bishop's Stand – Rousby Hall Road Angela Bishop (pictured) has owned and operated this food stand since 1950.

St. John's United Methodist Church – 1475 Soller's Wharf Road
One of the oldest Methodist churches (1829) transferred to Black congregation in 1880. Ruins of the previous church can still be seen.

Solomons
Calvert Marine Museum – 14200 Solomon's Island Road Alexander Butler (pictured) was an African American boat captain who lived near Planter's Wharf on St. Leonard Creek. Despite losing an arm as child, he became a successful schooner captain (hauling freight) in the early 1930's. Captain Butler may have been the only African American in Calvert County town and operate his own freight boat, the "W. H. French."

J. C. Lore Oysterhouse – 14430 Solomon's Island Road Seafood packing plant employed many African Americans in the 1930's and 40's (pictured); jobs ranged from working in the shipping yard to oystering, fishing and shucking.

Complete history at the J. C. Lore Oysterhouse

Lost images - Images of some buildings could not be located. They included ; "The Cozy", "The Hall", "Knotty Pine Bar and Grill", "Spinning Wheel", "Mabel Hawkins store" and several other "Mom and Pop" stores. Also listed as Colored owned in the 1928 business directory were; "Willetts Garage", "Earls", " Parran's store", "Lunch Room", "Gray's Filling station", " Masons confectionery", "Wallace's Grocery"," MT. Harmony Lunchroom", and "Scales Lunch Room".

EPILOGUE
The Final Battle

Blacks were the majority population in Calvert County up until the1970's. Multiple factors caused a population shift. Young people, both Black and White, turned away from farming and fishing. Calvert became a bedroom community for the Federal government in nearby Washington D.C.
A zoning war has been ongoing between those who want to "Keep Calvert Country" and those who want it more Urban. As a result, some of the zoning changes made it difficult for Young people to stay in Calvert. There were very few apartment complexes or Trailer parks. It even became more difficult and expensive to build on family owned land.

Family owned land became more difficult to retain as changes to the probate laws required families to act quickly to transfer title or risk losing track of heirs whose signatures were needed. Large homes built next to small homes caused property taxes to substantially increase. Most importantly for County natives, they would often have to leave Calvert in order to date someone that was not their cousin.

The final battle will be convincing young people to stay in Calvert. Hopefully learning how deep their roots run in the area will help. But even those who leave should take away the knowledge of how much energy and intelligence their ancestors used to survive and thrive through slavery, segregation, and racism.

To learn more:
Persistence, Perseverance and Progress: African American Education in Calvert County, Maryland, 1865-1965, Calvert County Government, 1996

The Money Crop: Tobacco Culture in Calvert County, Maryland, Maryland Historical and Cultural Publications and the Calvert County Historic District Commission 1992

Working the Water: the Commercial Fisherie of Maryland's Patuxent River, Calvert Marine Museum and the University Press of Virginia, Charlottesville, 1988.

Tribute to Calvert County African American World War II Veterans, Calvert County NAACP 2010

They Look Like Men of War! Calvert County's Colored Civil War Heroes, Calvert County NAACP 2011

Re-affirming Education as the Path to Freedom, Calvert County Branch of the Tourism, the Calvert Marine Museum.

Michael Gayhart Kent

Michael Gayhart Kent, one of six children of Gayhart and Viola Kent, was born in Calvert County in 1957. The family roots in Calvert can be traced to 1780. In 1839, my great - grandfather Benjamin Kent was born to his slave mother Susan and his White slave owner father, James P. King.
Also born in 1839 was George Armstrong Custer. Benjamin and his wife Rachel had sixteen children who are responsible for more than 2,000 descendants. It is my belief that these former slaves had a greater impact on U.S. history than many well-known Historical figures like Custer. Each successive generation focused on getting their children as much education as possible.
My education started at the segregated Mt. Hope elementary school. Our principal was Harriet Elizabeth Brown who would later be recognized by the State of Maryland for helping obtain equal pay for Colored teachers in 1937. As a result of the desegregation efforts, I attended multiple schools.

The first school I attended with White classmates was Mt. Harmony for the 5th and 6th grades. Junior high school (grades 7 and 8) as it was then called was renamed the Prince Frederick Middle school. From there, it was Calvert Senior high school for the 9th grade and Northern high school for grades 10 thru 12. Our class of 1975 was the first graduating class from Northern High. After high school, I continued my education for one year at Lincoln University in Pennsylvania. I left Lincoln to join the Navy Reserves and train as a Signalman. Upon completing training, I returned to college at the University of Maryland College Park and graduated with a B.A. in English. I then entered Law school at the University of Maryland in Baltimore. Simultaneously, I was commissioned an Ensign in the Navy Judge Advocate General's Corp. While on summer break from school, I obtained a certificate in computer programming from Catholic University in Washington D.C. During the summer, while assigned to active duty at the Nava base in Warminster Pennsylvania, I obtained certificates from Penn State University Abington campus, and also Temple University in Philadelphia. I also completed one semester of graduate work at the Wharton School of business at the University of Pennsylvania in Philadelphia. Another summer was spent at the Naval War College in Norfolk Virginia, before going on active duty on several ships.

During, the Fall and Spring I continued to attend law school at night while clerking for both the State's Attorney in Prince George's County (child support division) and the State's Attorney for Baltimore city (traffic division). After Law school, I worked as an Assistant State's Attorney for both Baltimore and Prince George's Counties. I also did contractual work for the Federal Public Defender's office. Upon returning to Calvert County, my interest in learning family history and local history increased. I was able to use some Oral histories to find supporting documents at the State archives, Court records, church records, and private family collections. It is my goal to preserve Calvert County's Black history and to make sure future generations know it. I disseminate as much information as possible by working with Calvert County School, Calvert County Public library, Calvert historical society, the N.A.A.C.P. and the Maryland Commission for African American History and Culture and the Calvert County Historic District Commission.

Made in the USA
Middletown, DE
24 February 2023